ישיבה תורת חיים

Yeshiva Toras Chaim
Talmudical Seminary/Denver
1400 Quitman Street • P.O. Box 4067
Denver, Colorado 80204
(303) 629-8200

Toras Chaim: Perpetuating Our Heritage

The strength of our people has always been the Torah, which was given to us at Mt. Sinai. The Torah, our heritage, forms the foundation of Jewish life and spirit. Torah study is not an endeavor limited to any specific moment or location, but, rather, a primary objective in Jewish living at any time and in any place.

"Study is the life-breath of the Jewish people, the goal of Jewish existence — its purpose and destiny," stated the sainted Rabbi Aaron Kotler, teacher and mentor of the men who head Yeshiva Toras Chaim Talmudical Seminary/Denver. The Yeshiva was founded in 1967 on the solid rock of Torah precepts. It was the first Yeshiva high school and college level Hebrew studies program between the Mississippi River and the West Coast. With its foundation firmly established, Yeshiva Toras Chaim began its upward growth.

Over the years, Yeshiva Toras Chaim has demonstrated dedication and commitment — a commitment, not only to the individual development and spiritual growth of each student in the school, but a commitment to transmit our special heritage by reaching out to Jewish youth and community leaders, as well as to lay people, professionals and business people. The Yeshiva offers varied Torah learning programs in order to appeal to many segments of Denver's Jewish community. A superior well-spring of Torah knowledge is available through the Yeshiva. Jewish scholars share their knowledge with those who wish to find their Jewish roots or expand their Jewish intellectual horizons.

In addition to its on-going programs, the Yeshiva has joined in a worldwide effort to make possible the emigration of Soviet Jewry, by accepting a group of young Russian students from Kishinev, Moldavia. They arrived under a landmark foreign exchange program approved by the government of Moldavia that will allow youth from the Soviet republic to travel to the West to study. The Yeshiva is not only providing for all of their physical needs, but, more importantly, is bringing these young Russian students back to their own precious, spiritual Torah heritage, as well.

Yeshiva Toras Chaim is proud to participate in the publication of this special exclusive edition of Moshe Holczler's "Late Memories," a moving autobiographical account of the spiritual heroism during the dark days of the Holocaust. We hope this book will help to increase the awareness of the suffering and plight of the Holocaust victims, and serve as a reminder of the struggle of our people for so many generations. We trust you and your family will find this book a source of inspiration and personal edification.

MOSHE HOLCZLER'S

LATE
MEMORIES

■ ■ ■

CIS
P·U·B·L·I·S·H·E·R·S
New York · London · Jerusalem

Copyright © 1991

All rights reserved.
This book, or any part thereof,
may not be reproduced in any
form whatsoever without the express
written permission of the copyright holder.

Published and distributed
in the U.S., Canada and overseas by
C.I.S. Publishers and Distributors
180 Park Avenue, Lakewood, New Jersey 08701
(908) 905-3000 Fax: (908) 367-6666

Distributed in Israel by
C.I.S. International (Israel)
Rechov Mishkalov 18
Har Nof, Jerusalem
Tel:02-538-935

Distributed in the U.K. and Europe by
C.I.S. International (U.K.)
1 Palm Court, Queen Elizabeth Walk
London, England N16
Tel: 01-809-3723

Cover design: Joseph Neumark
Typography: Nechamie Miller

Cover illustration reproduced
from original painting by Francis McGinley

ISBN 1-56062-070-6 soft cover

PRINTED IN THE UNITED STATES OF AMERICA

Dedicated in Memory of

R' Mendel Shapiro

הוקדש לז"נ

ר' ישראל מנחם ב"ר ברוך זאב ז"ל

נפטר הושענא רבה תשנ"א

Amid the horrors of the Warsaw ghetto
and the other concentration camps in Poland,
he kept his commitment to Shmiras Hamitzvos.

Although he lost his own two children,
he walked the pathways of life
with an enduring faith and a radiant joy.

He came to a new world,
but the spirit of the glorious years of Polish Jewry
throbbed within him all his life.

He maintained his eternal loyalties,
and the concern for Gmilas Chasodim to others
was always his primary focus.

With everlasting and loving appreciation
by his devoted wife,
Mrs. Ruth Shapiro

ולעילוי נשמות בתם ובנם הקדושים

פיינה מחלה בת ר' ישראל מנחם הי"ד

יצחק מאיר שלמה ב"ר ישראל מנחם הי"ד

תנצב"ה

Dedicated in Loving Memory
of Our Husband, Father and Grandfather

Israel (Srul) Ruda

הוקדש לז״נ

ר׳ ישראל בן יצחק שלמה ז״ל

נפטר י״ד שבט תשנ״א

In the Warsaw ghetto his care and concern
for the well being of others were legendary.

He was humble and unassuming, yet strong in spirit,
a man of forthright character and integrity.

A most devoted husband and father,
he was always sensitive to the needs of others
and found pleasure in making everyone happy.

His kindness and love of Yiddishkeit
will be remembered by his children
and grandchildren for posterity.

by

Mrs. Sylvia Ruda

Eva and Ronn Hull

Jacques and Lisa Ruda
Emily, Charles & Shauna

Joyce and Jay Moskowitz
Elisheva & Avigayil

הוקדש לז"נ

ר' אלעזר אליהו ב"ר ראובן הכהן ז"ל

נפטר ח' ניסן תש"ה

ומרת טושנה בת ר' בונם ע"ה

נפטרה ח' תמוז תשל"ח

למשפחת שפיצער

☆ ☆ ☆

הוקדש לז"נ

ר' יצחק ב"ר יששכר הכהן קליין ז"ל

נפטר ר"ח אב תשמ"א

☆ ☆ ☆

הוקדש לז"נ

ר' חיים אליעזר ב"ר ישראל גלאק ז"ל

נפטר ו' כסלו תשמ"ו

☆ ☆ ☆

הוקדש לז"נ

ר' ראובן ב"ר אלעזר אליהו הכהן שפיצער ז"ל

נפטר י' טבת תשנ"א

Table of Contents

■ ■ ■

Publisher's Note 11
Introduction 17
The Core of Life 25
Memories of My Childhood 30
For My Father's Sake 38
The Last Section of the Fence 56
The Germans Invade 63
A Mission of Rescue 68
Air Raid over Budapest 89
The Margit Bridge 98
Do You Have Seven Pennies? .104
Light Signals 108
Five Minutes of Chanukah 113
My Friend Erzsi 121
A Lump of Sugar 124
The Night in the Forest 129
How to Survive a Survival 137
A Firebrand Lives 153
The White Armband 160
Those Little Shoes 176
A Minchah in the Air 181

Publisher's Note

■ ■ ■

NEARLY HALF A CENTURY HAS PASSED SINCE THE CLOSE OF THE
darkest chapter in history, when six million innocent Jewish
men, women and children perished in the Nazi holocaust. In
the century of greatest technological advancement, of osten-
sible social and political enlightenment of revolutionary pro-
portions, the human race plumbed the most abysmal depths
of barbarism, infinitely greater than any previously unleashed
on civilization. The crime committed against the holy Jewish
people by the German demons in earthly form was so hei-
nous, so monstrous that it attains an almost mystical level of
evil, like a ghastly satanic force released from the nethermost
reaches of Hell. It was a crime beyond vengeance, beyond
mundane retribution, a crime that has no venue other than the
Heavenly Court and whose victims must look inward to find
some meaning in an unfathomable experience.

The tragedy that befell the Jewish people was profound,
pervasive and indiscriminate to a truly unimaginable degree,

and it left in its wake a number of staggering philosophical and sociological questions. Undoubtedly, many of these questions must remain unanswered and unanswerable, but perhaps now, when in the broad contexts of history we are at least a few paces removed from the event, when the passage of time has dulled the razor's edge of the hellish agonies suffered by our people, perhaps now we can attempt to form a perspective which we can pass on to future generations as the legacy of these times.

It is accepted without question that we must record the awful events of the holocaust as an everlasting testimony for posterity. To this end, a whole genre of literature has emerged which chronicles the Jewish experiences during these years in painstaking and excruciatingly painful detail, but somehow, when all is said and done, this secular holocaust literature falls short of the mark.

After we have read all the heartrending stories of the atrocities and the sadism and the suffering and the systematic extermination, after we have turned the last page and shed the last tear, what remains with us, what do we take back with us into our everyday existence? If our responsibility to remember is so axiomatic, what then is the purpose of this eternal memorialization? Are we to remember in order to prevent a recurrence of this tragedy? How? By appealing to the conscience of the gentile world? Bitter experience has taught us the futility of such hopes. Is it then to allow us to escape if the ugly Nazi death's-head is lifted up again, *chas vechalilah*? Surely, it is naive to expect more than a small number of individuals to grasp the opportunity to abandon home and hearth, while the majority remain immobilized by helpless optimism. Is it then simply a dutiful memory without purpose, without meaning? Does such a remembrance do justice to those we must remember?

To this end, Judaica holocaust literature does give substance and meaning to the memories we must record for

posterity. There can be no doubt that the holocaust period was brought on by a colossal outburst of Divine Wrath, and although we cannot precisely pinpoint the cause of this Wrath, as our Prophet and Sages were able to do with earlier cataclysms, a brief comparison of the pre-War and post-War period offers some inklings. During the first part of this century, European Jewry was mortally infected by rampant *haskalah*, socialism and secular zionism to such a degree that young people were abandoning traditional Judaism in droves and the citadel of Torah was rapidly crumbling; even those strongholds of Torah and Yiddishkeit, such as the great *yeshivos* and *Chassidic* centers, were fighting heroically but defensively against the gathering tide.

In the wake of the holocaust, however, the trends have paradoxically reversed. The pernicious ideologies are discredited and in decline, and Torah flourishes as seldom before in a staunch Jewish society rebuilt by holocaust survivors. Clearly, in the broader national consciousness, the tragedy of the holocaust awakened and reinvigorated a dormant spiritual fortitude upon whose foundation the new Jewish world was erected.

Now, as we look back after fifty years, we can see this clearly, yet we cannot help but wonder at the pain and suffering of the pure and innocent. Once again, we are faced with the age-old anomaly of "*rasha ve'tov lo, tzaddik ve'ra lo*," only this time on an unprecedented cosmic scale where perhaps the conventional responses do not quite suffice. But even if we cannot find a satisfactory answer, we must accept it without question and without an erosion of our faith.

Judaica holocaust literature teaches us that the holocaust was a war between the Jewish people and the German Amalek-incarnate. It was a war of the carnal brute against the sublime spirit, of the violent against the gentle, the godless against the devout, the profane against the holy. And in the end, the Jewish people emerged victorious, because the

Germans could only destroy our bodies but not our souls and spirits.

The only true Jewish casualties, in the fullest sense of the word, were those who turned against their faith, although it would be unconscionable for us, who sit in the comfort and safety of our own times, to judge and condemn them. It was these people who went to their slaughter in utter despair and defeat. Those people, however, who went to their deaths with a song of undying faith on their lips, the true *kedoshim*, were ultimately victorious in their knowledge that they were infinitely above their savage German tormentors. And those who survived, whose rocklike faith and devotion to the *Ribono Shel Olam* and His Torah were tested and forged in the fiercest crucible that ever descended on the face of the earth, those are the true heroes who emerged from this holocaust stronger and greater than ever before and who went on to rebuild a new and better Jewish world on the ashes of the old.

It is the testimony of these people that we must hear and record for all future generations. Their priceless words, and the exalted spirit with which they are infused, are the ultimate legacy of these dreadful times. This then is what we must remember, that in the darkest moments in the lowest pit of Hell, the faith in their hearts shone perhaps more brightly than ever before, and it shone with such a powerful light that it will still illuminate our world long after they have passed on to a better world. Out of this faith there also emerges a wondrous hope that in the midst of the holocaust, which etymologically means a total conflagration, one is never beyond hope, that the *Ribono Shel Olam* hears the prayers of the individual and performs miracles for him, and indeed, there are virtually no survivors who were not saved numerous times by miracles, whether or not they recognized them as such.

These are the thoughts that come to the fore as we launch this collection of holocaust memoirs entitled *The Holocaust*

Diaries. While all holocaust literature written from a Torah perspective is valuable and eminently worthy of publication, we have attempted in this collection to select and present the memoirs of survivors of transcendent spirit who are the very stuff of history, whose lives and thoughts and feelings are worthy of being held up as a shining example for all future generations. In this endeavor, we feel fortunate and honored to have as our inaugural volume the memoirs and impressions of Moshe Holczler entitled *Late Shadows*. Subsequent to *Late Shadows*, we have also had the honor of publishing *They Called Me Frau Anna* by Chana Marcus Banet, the deeply moving memoir of a valiant woman who wandered through war-ravaged Poland with her two small children until she found refuge as a housekeeper for a high-ranking Nazi official. Three other major works are currently in preparation. *Counterfeit Lives* by Avraham Krakowski, a memoir of exile in Siberia by Dina Gabel and a translation of the classic *Ich Vel Zei Iberleiben* by Chaim Shlomo Friedman. We welcome and invite submissions of similar autobiographical works, and we are prepared to work closely with the authors in presenting their memories and thoughts to the general reading public and in the benefit of posterity.

This volume, *Late Memories* is an excerpt from *Late Shadows*, where it appears as the first of the seven sections of this monumental work. It is the personal story of Moshe Holczler and his wife Sarah. Some chapters in this section have been written by Sarah Holczler from her perspective, and the authorship of each individual chapter is indicated. We have also added several chapters culled from other sections of *Late Shadows*, such as *Late Reactions* and *Late Encounters*, as respectively indicated.

At this point, I would like to extend a note of gratitude and appreciation, on behalf of all of us at C.I.S. Publishers, to Mr. and Mrs. Holczler for their gracious cooperation in the laborious process of selecting, assembling, revising and compiling

Late Shadows. It was a great pleasure and honor to work with them, and we wish them continued good fortune, long life, health and much happiness. I would also like to offer a special note of recognition to Administrative Editor Raizy Kaufman, originator and project coordinator of *The Holocaust Diaries*. Her foresight, enthusiasm and perseverance were instrumental in the successful launching of this endeavor, and her meticulous efforts in the compilation and organization of the intricate *Late Shadows*, the book from which this excerpt is drawn, are manifest in its final form.

In closing, I would like to offer a prayer to the *Ribono Shel Olam* that He look upon our work with favor and bless our efforts with success, so that the memoirs of these noble-spirited people may be eternally preserved and bring honor to His Name and solace to His downtrodden people.

Y.Y.R.
Lakewood, N.J.
Nissan, 5751

Introduction

■ ■ ■

AS I SIT DOWN TO WRITE THESE WORDS, MY THOUGHTS GO BACK
to a particular day in the fall of 1938. Coming home from the
morning sessions of the Jozsef Nador Technical University of
Budapest, I was in a very despondent mood. Tipped of by a
sympathetic gentile student, I had just escaped within a
hairsbreadth of falling victim to an organized attack against
the Jewish students, an attack that was scheduled to erupt at
eleven o'clock recess, right after the mathematics session. I
had enrolled in the school only reluctantly, because of pressure from Jewish community leaders, and now I was being
driven away like an inferior stranger who was intruding in a
place where he did not belong.

In my rage, I decided never to return there again. I was
hurt in my human self-consciousness and disillusioned with
the world of supposedly pure science; if bigotry and discrimi-
nation existed in the world of higher research, what value
could it have?

Of course, when I told the Jewish community leaders who had urged me to attend that I had decided not to return, they were extremely indignant. How could I think of such a step when I was one of only four Jewish students in all Hungary admitted that year to the University? Did I not feel an obligation to my Jewish fellows as a whole? Nonetheless, I adamantly refused to return, pointing out that if Jews would remain within their own culture and concentrate on the study of the Torah, they would not be subjected to such indignities.

The next day, when I returned from the morning prayers, my mother greeted me with a warm smile.

"You had an important telephone call," she told me. "The president of the Jewish Rescue Center in Budapest called. He wants you to be the manager of a new district office in our neighborhood."

Me to manage a rescue office, a field with which I was unfamiliar? And what gave them the idea to turn to me? Was this perhaps some new hint from Heaven with regards to which direction my life should take?

I called and made an appointment for the early afternoon hours. My meeting with the president, a dignified man in his late fifties, was an experience by itself. He leaned back in his leather armchair and looked at me with encouragement.

"We need you," he said. "We know about your educational background both in our own sacred treasures and in the secular fields. You are surely aware of the Anti-Jewish Law which has already ruined and impoverished hundreds of Jewish families all around the country. Well, a second law is in the making, and by next spring, it is expected to pass both houses of parliament. If that comes to pass, thousands of Jewish families will be left penniless. To defend against this possibility, we have formed OMZSA, Country-wide Hungarian Jewish Rescue Action, through which, with the help of international funding, we are working to have it's impact reduced. We are organizing a new district center in your neighborhood, and we thought it would be a good idea to draft you as our manager. We need your abilities. You would receive a decent salary, of course. So what do you think?"

I was really flabbergasted. It was a challenge, but was I really suited to the task?

"Please tell me what made you call just me?" I asked. "What makes you feel that I would be suitable to such a role?"

"Well," the president replied. "I heard you had quit the university because of the anti-Semitic terror . . . and I liked that! We must have self-pride in this hate-storm or we will be completely lost."

For a while, I was engulfed in deep thoughts; his words had touched my innermost feelings. It would be an entirely new horizon in my life, and I would be dealing with people and their fate.

"I will try it," I said. "Let's see how it works out."

My acceptance was followed by a grateful and reassuring handshake. This handshake decided the direction of my life for long years to come.

This was the first of four occasions that life put me in the path of helping alleviate Jewish suffering. The second was after the war in Oradea Mare as manager of the Refugee Receiving Station. The third was with the Agudath Israel office in Budapest, and the fourth was in the United States where I have headed the Targem Restitution Office since 1959.

At my Targem office, I have to listen to the stories of persecutees in order to help them present their cases to the Germans. I have to inquire for the details of their mental and physical sufferings. One's heart would have to be of stone not to break when listening to these first-hand reports. Somehow, these people instinctively sense that they find a sympathetic ear with me, and they open up. Often, especially with the more dramatic reports, I would record their reports and put them in my file. Already, the thought of one day putting them together in book form was percolating in my mind, and now at last, eight years later, that dream has come true. These records, extensively re-edited and revised, supplemented and reorganized, as well as my own personal memories, comprise the bulk of *Late Shadows*.

This volume *Late Memories*, is an excerpt of *Late Shadows*, where it appears as the first part of the book. It tells our own story of miraculous escape, manifestations of heavenly help and human greatness stemming of unshakable faith and devotion. It is intended as a paean to G-d through whose unending kindness "the trap broke and we escaped," and as an expression of gratitude for our renewed lives and our children who grew up as a result of this escape. I have also included several chapters from other sections of *Late Shadows*.

Here I have to mention that I consulted a number of times with the Skverer Rebbe, may he live long, with regard to this book, describing in detail its essential goals and the names of our publishers, and I am happy to say that he gave his enthusiastic blessing for success and *nessias chein* with the general reading public.

My sincerest thanks and appreciation go to C.I.S. Publishers for their deep insight in embracing my works with the utmost sympathy and understanding. Their high standard and breadth of scope are furthering the development of reliable and valuable Judaica literature. I feel fortunate to have exactly the kind of individuals I always envisioned as my publishers. I immediately felt that I had come to the proper place with my writings, and this impression was only increased as our contacts became more frequent. I hope very profoundly that our partnership will be fruitful and long-lasting.

And now, last but not least, as I'm examining my work, I realize with some sadness that I may appear to my readers as the chronicler of destruction and suffering, whose only purpose in life is to commemorate and record doom, persecution and horror. Please, believe me that this is not so! It is forced upon me by the daily impressions of my occupations and by my human compassion for my people. But this is not my object in life!

I am a writer who is deeply interested in every manifestation of human soul, every facet of human emotions. I love hope, faith-filled joy, literary creation, moods and dramatic tensions. I strive to render moral value to all my writings, and I always endeavor to paint some "shiny spots" even onto the darkest stories, where the radiance of the soul can ultimately protrude. Instead of being remembered as a "late shadow," I would much prefer to become an "early sunshine" to everybody. Still, this sad role is part of my destiny, a destiny which fell upon me when I was entrusted with the sad stories of the tear-stained people sitting across my desk.

Hashem should give me strength and possibility to produce more cheerful and brighter writings, to uplift and enliven the spirit of my readers.

Moshe Holczler

MOSHE HOLCZLER'S
LATE MEMORIES

The Core of Life

■ ■ ■

Moshe Holczler

FOR FIVE GENERATIONS, MY FATHER'S ANCESTORS LIVED IN THE counties of Fejer and Pest near Budapest, the Hungarian capital. They were Oberlander (Ashkenazic) Jews, and they earned their living by trade. My father himself was an electrical contractor, specializing in urban projects.

My mother's family was from the region of Mezocsat, Heves and Erlau. Her grandfather was a *shochet* as well as a *Talmudic* scholar at the congregation of the famous Netai Soirek at Mezocsat. My mother was a teacher when she met my father.

Their marriage was delayed for years, due to the length and travail of the First World War. As soon as the war was over, they married, like many others at that time. At first they lived in a suburb of Budapest, where I was born. Shortly afterwards, my parents moved to Budapest, where I was raised.

My father was a good-hearted, polite and straightforward person. He was very talented, learned quickly, was ambitious and always played leading roles. He had a beautiful handwriting; "like a minister-president," we used to tell him. He was a good organizer, with many workers under his direction.

Unfortunately, life dealt him a bitter lot. After a happy marriage of about two years, my mother suddenly passed away while giving birth to her second child, my only sister. At that time, I was fifteen months old, and my poor father was forced to raise his two orphans by himself. My father's sorrow knew no limits. He neglected his business, trying his best to replace my mother, but he couldn't bear this burden alone for more than about two years. He was under constant pressure to marry again, which he finally did.

As you can imagine, I didn't know my mother or at least I didn't have any memories of her. All the years of my childhood, I had to collect memories from pictures, descriptions by family members and accounts of friends and neighbors. All I know is that her pictures contract my heart up to this very day with a sad sorrow and, at the same time, a deep, warm, unexplainable love. From the looks of her eyes, I could feel who she was, a warm, fine, intelligent person, with a faint sad smile around her lips and a painful faraway look in her eyes.

People tell me that everyone loved her, that she made them smile and was a source of solace in times of need or distress. The four long years of the First World War virtually stole her youth. She became a nurse, and when her own brother was injured by shrapnel, she sat at his sickbed for months, day and night, until he was out of danger. She was very happy with me, friends say, and there wasn't a prouder young mother in town. She let everybody look at her red-haired baby when on a stroll with the carriage and she looked forward to a long life of motherhood with great expectations.

Two and a half years after her tragic death, my father remarried a woman from the upper part of Slovakia. She came from the city of Kezmarok, the eldest girl in a family of twelve children. They were a very closely knit family, strictly religious, but with a tint of brightness and cultural orientation. They were always in the middle of local society. Her father was a bearded Jew, the head of an interstate moving company, who had moved with his family from the forests of Zakopane on the Polish side of the border and settled in Kezmarok.

Kezmarok was the center of the so-called "Zipserdeutsch" settlement in Slovakia. The dominant language was German. They had German newspapers and they lived a vivid, highly cultured community life. This combination of factors influenced my further upbringing a great deal.

Fortunately, my stepmother was like a natural mother to my sister and myself. She brought us up like her own children, with love and devotion. Until our early teens, respectively, we didn't know that she wasn't our real mother; my father and our family didn't want to disturb our developing minds. After having been told, I still loved her as before, because I appreciated her goodness so much. To this day, when I talk about her or think of her, I always call her my "second mother."

Every summer, she took us to Kezmarok for two or three months. Kezmarok was located under the High Tatras, an Alpine range of snow-clad mountains, crystal clear rivers and wide pine forests. We loved this experience after the suppressed air and jammed streets of the Hungarian capital, and it became our second home.

My second mother raised us to conform with her own upbringing, so I enjoyed a combination of strictly religious education along with a well-founded secular education as well. Furthermore, being in Kezmarok so often, the German language became my second native language, and this explains many developments in my further years, culminating in my *Wiedergutmachung* activities up to this day. In general, my day was composed of a morning of Torah study and a late afternoon of private secular studies, which included midterm and final exams at the local boy's Gymnasium. Thanks to this combination of studies, and to the private tutoring, I was able to advance to the point where I took the Graduate Exam, which I passed *summa cum laude*. Throughout all this, I remained deeply religious in essence and a devoted member of the Orthodox Jewish community of the capital.

I especially favored two subject areas, literature and the natural sciences. I believe that my inclination toward the natural world was inspired by my stepmother's habit of taking us to her beautiful country home under the High Tatras in Kezmarok each summer. That grand and fascinating group of snow-clad mountains kept me spellbound for years and implanted a great love in my heart for high mountains, scented pines and the mysterious splashing of mountain streams.

One particular summer morning during that period of my life stands out in my mind. I remember taking a blanket and a book and going up alone into a pasture hidden within the recesses of the high mountain peaks. I spread the blanket atop the knee-high grass and made a wild spot under a pine branch into an alcove all my own. I recall how that high grass was dappled with a dazzling variation of wildflower colors, like a fantastic carpet. I recall closing my eyes, my face flushed, my heart galloping from the quick climb in the thin air and the diligent sounds of butterflies and grasshoppers all around me. Everything was so full of life and beauty, I thanked G-d for having created such a wonderful world of which I could also be a part. I recall feeling such a tremendous sense of the core of life and such a deep gratitude for having life that I could only pray to and praise G-d my whole life long.

In retrospect, I would say that it was this love of life and beauty, which has been a part of me ever since, that gave me the strength and courage to fight for my life when it was threatened. I considered life a privilege which no one but the One who gave it could take away.

In June of 1938, I was admitted to the Polytechnical University of Budapest, to my great surprise. It seems that my academic record was of sufficient caliber to allow me to be

one of four Jews in Hungary to be admitted. I was not enthusiastic about the prospect. When I applied under Jewish
community pressure, I was so sure that I wouldn't be admitted
that I was shocked when I was accepted. At first, I refused to
go because I feared I would be endangering my religious life,
but my refusal was met with such consternation on the part of
the Jewish Educational Alliance in Budapest that I did not
know what to do. They insisted that it would be selfish of me
to let such an opportunity slip by. It then occurred to me that
attendance at the university might help me avoid being
drafted into the forced labor battalions of the army. That
thought finally made me decide to go. Later it turned out that
my university I.D. Card was the only document I could use at
my escape from the army and getting back to Budapest.

Six months after my arrival at the University, the rabidly
anti-Semitic Turul Society had organized open attacks upon
Jewish students, demanding a "Jew-free" university. When I
was told by a friendly student that an attack against the Jews
was to take place after the math professor left the room, I
escaped by means of the service stairway and never returned.

In October of 1938, I became manager of a district office
of the new Hungarian Jewish Rescue Committee, called
OMZSA. That organization was formed to counteract the
tragic loss of Jewish livelihood brought on by the Anti-Jewish
Laws which undercut the economic position of thousands of
Hungarian Jews. This was the first time I had to face Jewish
suffering daily and was required to use all of my abilities to
help my fellow Jews.

I stayed at that position for four years, during which time
I was wholly occupied with my duties, and then I was drafted
into one of the forced labor battalions. I had no choice but to
go, and I left my position very sadly, as if I was abandoning my
charge and responsibilities.

Memories of My Childhood

■ ■ ■

Sarah Holczler

I WAS BORN AND RAISED IN SALGTARJAN, A SMALL TOWN IN Hungary in which my grandfather started a wholesale coal business, later inherited by my father. I never actually saw the coal until my early teenage years, and I believed that our occupation was doing *mitzvos*.

My father launched his "*mitzvah* business" after marrying my mother and bringing her home from Budapest. My grandfather's house was like Avraham Avinu's house, with *orchim* and *bachurim* constant house guests, and his sons continued the family tradition. In this respect, my father was the most outstanding, because his *maasim tovim* were his constant occupation.

In describing my father's family, one picture stands out in my memory. I was a little girl, and as usual, we were at our Bubby's house. There was great excitement, because the family was being visited by my uncle from Balassagyarmat, a nearby city. My uncle was a respected *talmid chacham*,

30

dayan and *shochet*. When he arrived, he bent down and kissed his father's hand. I saw the two long beards intermingling, only my grandfather's was whiter. Suddenly, my beloved aunt rushed out from the kitchen, bowed and kissed her brother's hand.

"Auntie, why did you kiss your brother's hand?" I asked my aunt later on in the day.

"I kissed his Torah!" was the smiling answer.

My mother was the fifteenth child of her parents. She was born in Paks, Hungary, where her parents owned a few inns and distilleries. She was brought up in comfort and love. When most of the children were married, my grandfather decided to fulfill his lifelong dream of emigrating to Jerusalem, where he wanted to devote his remaining years strictly to Torah learning. In this desire, he was greatly influenced by his lifelong *chaver* Rav Duschinsky who also emigrated to Jerusalem. My grandmother, who was a descendent of a long line of *rabbonim*, was an equal partner in this aspiration. As they still had three unmarried sons, they took them along to Eretz Yisrael. Only my mother remained behind in Hungary, because she had an insurance policy which had been taken out by her parents for the purpose of providing her with a dowry, and the policy stipulated that upon her twentieth birthday she personally apply for the insurance money. The year was 1912. At that time my mother was eighteen years old, and even though she was heart-broken about it, she had to remain with her married sisters and wait out the two years until she could join her parents in Jerusalem.

Finally, after endless yearning and crying, the waiting came to an end. Everything went according to the plan. She got her money and made preparations for the journey to Jerusalem. She traveled to her numerous brothers and sisters, who all lived in different towns, to say good-bye, when . . . the First World War broke out! She was stranded! Waiting hopelessly for the war to end, she finally married in the third year of the war, 1917. As it turned out, ten more years were to pass before she would visit her dear parents in Jerusalem.

Many decaded later, after I lost my parents in Auschwitz, I had the *zchus* to stand by my maternal grandparents' *kever* on Har Hazeisim and read the inscription on my grandfather's tombstone: *Reb Mordechai Yehudah Herzl, talmid legaonim hatzaddikim Reb Menachem Ash v'Hakesav Sofer, zichronom livrocho.*

We were only two sisters, one year apart, but with very different natures. While my sister was pretty and ladylike, I resembled my father and was boyish and wild. We loved our gentle mother deeply. Her main and unending concern was her children. She was a romantic soul and her care for us was meticulous. Later, an older cousin remarked, "It's a wonder you didn't become spoiled monsters!" But nobody knew that under the very refined, soft-spoken mother, there was a very strict educator. Her gentleness carried a steely firmness if we veered from good manners or behaved mischievously.

The little town in which we lived was my beloved sphere; its streets housed my uncles, aunts and cousins. We spent most of our waking hours in grandmother's yard. Her six-family house contained dozens of cousins, and we were always playing with them. It was certainly more fun than in our quiet, orderly house.

The town's population was about twenty thousand. There were about seventy or eighty Orthodox families, a small minority compared to even the non-Orthodox, whom we called Neolog.

Before we reached school-age, one of the non-Orthodox leaders sold the Jewish school to the city. We therefore had no choice but to go to public school. After six elementary grades, many of the Orthodox girls were taken home, their compulsory schooling completed. As I was a straight-A student, my father had to bend to my pleading, fortified by the school director, to let me continue on. And so, my sister and I went to junior high school for another four years.

When *Yaamim Tovim* arrived, we were free from school. School time continued, however, and we were obligated to make up the missed lessons. Several of the gentile girls were friendly and willing to help, encouraged by the school authorities. It was not unusual for us to be friendly with gentile girls when we were very young since our grandparents' house shared yard space with gentile houses, but we strongly felt the difference between us and did not become overly close. Junior high studies took me into better gentile homes when we had to supplement missing *Yom Tov* lessons. I was graciously received and helped, yet I always detected a somewhat condescending attitude.

In my last year of school, I was the only Jewish girl still attending. To my happy surprise, I received a merit award at the graduation ceremonies. The school authorities wanted to show their unbiased standing. I cried myself to sleep that night, knowing that I was finished with formal schooling and already missing school terribly.

At that time, my grandfather passed away and my father took over the family business. He needed help, and my sister and I were expected to assist. Helping my father put me into a very active role. I was constantly rushing through the length of Main Street to reach the coal depot, where I supervised the coal delivery to horse-drawn wagons. Our town was a center of coal mining and many other factories as well.

Along Main Street, all the stores were owned by Jews. They were all my friends and acquaintances. If I left town for a short visit elsewhere, they welcomed me warmly on my homecoming. The clerks at the post office were eager to hear where I had been. It was home to me.

My public school background, contact with gentile families and schoolmates and my business contacts brought me closer to the non-Jewish population. I was also quite friendly with some non-Orthodox girls, whose outlook to the "other side" was broadminded. We loved humanity. In this spirit, I caused my father plenty of worry. He would have been happier with a simple, uncomplicated girl for a daughter. He was constantly concerned about my incessant reading and associations with "over-educated" girls.

My father was a very forceful, rather stern man, whom we loved, admired but also feared. He watched over the entire community, taking care of all the poor people and helping them in every way. He would not accept any religious transgression from anyone, certainly not from his own daughters. We did not wish to give him any worry, and in our opinion we were very *frum* girls. Still, many times we felt that if not for our mother's gentle understanding, we would have been shut off from his life completely.

My first rude awakening to anti-Semitism came from the following episode. At the time, Jews were still rightful citizens, although Hungary was becoming increasingly friendly with Germany and as such expected difficulties with the Western powers. There was preparation for impending war, and bomb shelters were being constructed. We even planned our own shelter in our back yard.

Citizens were organized into civil defense. There were groups watching the skies every night, using powerful reflectors to detect any enemy planes flying into our area. For this vigil, the leader of the civil defense recruited girls over sixteen years of age and assigned them to public buildings overnight. I was assigned with some twenty other girls, mostly Catholic, to a casino building. We were quite safe, and we made friends and entertained each other as we had very little to do. From time to time, we went out into the courtyard in pairs and watched the sky. Later on, we decided to go to sleep, taking turns on the table tops and chairs. We were taught to be loyal citizens, and I remember feeling proud to be one of the patriotic group.

Halfway into the night, we heard loud, drunken singing

from the corridor outside our door. It became harsher and rougher, and to my horror, I recognized it as a bloodthirsty Nazi song depicting the Jews as pigs for slaughter. I could not contain my anger, and I wanted to know who dared sing it here. I ran to the door and saw a staggering young man. I recognized him as the fiance of one of my schoolmates, who had been introduced to me a few months previously. He was employed at the railroad station, and since I had to travel often, he frequently saw me and greeted me with friendliness.

I could not believe and accept this. I remember looking into those savage eyes as I screamed, "What are you doing singing this anti-Semitic horror? You are a normal man!"

He bent over and hissed into my ears, "I want to kill you! All of you! The time has arrived. You will not escape me!"

By that time, the girls were curiously surrounding me and snickering, saying, "He is drunk. Don't hold him responsible."

We brought in the watchman, who pulled him away.

I crept back inside, completely shattered by the experience. There went my universal love for mankind.

As the anti-Semitic waves started to wash over us, our business connections with the biggest coal mining company became shaky. Even before the Anti Jewish Laws, the big powerful companies started to dismiss Jews from high positions. As we were the exclusive agency to sell their coal in two counties, my father had to have personal contact with them quite often. Being a bearded Jew, he felt uncomfortable in their offices, which we called "the Palace." To my utter shock, my father requested that my sister and I take over his role. We felt very young, and the weight of the responsibility was overwhelming.

It was true that a young girl was usually more welcome than a Jew with a beard, even though my father always had a well-trimmed beard and wore neckties. Nonetheless, his jackets were a bit longer than fashionable, and where he was respected and welcome before, he now received nasty remarks. The older directors were mostly replaced by hostile Nazi sympathizers.

These enormous new responsibilities changed me from a carefree, literary girl to a serious grownup.

On one occasion when I had to go to "the Palace," I timidly knocked on the door of the director, knowing fully the importance of my mission. When I entered, the fat old director did not even bother to accept my greeting, not to mention offering a chair, as on previous occasions. I therefore remained close to the door with deference, patiently awaiting admission which did not come. I was not accepted but not sent away, either.

After shifting positions on my feet several times, I became very angry. I took my writing pad from my pocketbook and started drawing the director's face. I made the double chin comfortably well-rounded, eliminating the double fold, as well as the pouches under his eyes due to his heavy drinking. I drew a generally younger face. All this time, he ignored my presence. He just continued scribbling something on his desk. After I was satisfied with my hasty drawing, making sure the resemblance was striking, I ventured forth and placed the drawing in front of his face. Seconds passed as he studied the picture, and then a grin broke out on the stern face.

He began to laugh and said, "Won't you sit down? What can I do for you?"

I came forward and sat down.

"Did you study drawing?" he asked. When I said that I hadn't, he advised me to do so.

Finally, we came to the point. I ordered a large amount of coal for our waiting customers. It was promptly accepted, and with a flourish, he signed my order. I flew home on wings, saying *Tehillim* all the way.

After a blissful period with business as usual, we were notified that the mining company had appointed someone else as their representative. Our business was finished.

For a while, I became a kindergarten teacher upon the advice of our *rebbe*, who was a very close friend of our family. He pointed out that it would be a great *chessed*, as all the fathers were in forced labor camp and the mothers were taking care of the little children alone. I spent a little time in another town where I studied how to handle and teach little children. I was never especially talented in this vocation, but my violin playing helped. They loved it.

Often in my memories, I am visited by these beautiful, innocent little faces. These children were always freshly washed, wearing starched petticoats and silk bows in their shiny hair. Pretty little children . . . all killed by the Nazi beasts.

For My Father's Sake

■ ■ ■

Moshe Holczler

WE WERE STATIONED IN A REMOTE ROMANIAN VILLAGE WITH MY
Hungarian army labor detachment. It was the city of Varadcsechi, on a mountaintop overlooking the valley of Oradea
Mare. This village was near the border with Romania, and our
task was to clear the border forest for the regular patrol troops
and to cut a deployment strip below the immediate border for
eventual army intervention.

We were quartered in very primitive peasant houses and
slept on dirt floors covered with straw. There were no chairs
or tables. Every chore had to be done on the floor. Our clothes
were our own, short pants and sporty shirts. The caps and
boots were supplied by the army, as were the yellow stripes
on our left arms. Our tools were short and very sharp hatchets,
which hung from our belts. We carried heavy, long-handled
axes on our shoulders.

Our daily work started at eight A.M., at which time we
already had to be at our place of work. We were awakened at

five thirty A.M., and fifteen minutes later we had to line up for the morning coffee and marmalade with our mess tins. The yard where we stood was filled with the indignant muttering and cursing of shivering boys awakened from their deepest slumber at this early hour.

We left Varadcsechi in formation towards our work places. Not far from the village, we had to enter a dense, unfriendly and forbidding pine forest. As we arrived at the other side of the forest, the first rays of the rising sun illuminated the tree trunks, and a railroad embankment obstructed our path. To our right was an underpass. At this point, we were always ordered to stop, and everyone had to straighten his outfit before we crossed over into a very prestigious mountain spa of Felixfurdo.

On the top of the embankment stood a two-coach motor train, and almost every day, just as we crossed this underpass, the familiar trumpet of the conductor gave the final signal for the first train to go. As the train rumbled out above our heads, we entered the quiet elegance of a modern little country establishment, wedged into the gigantic mountainside, surrounded by scented pine forests, swishing mountain streams and a magnificent lake. We had to hold our breaths in wonder at the great contrast between our muddy Romanian village and these elegant, colorful hotels and bath houses lined with brightly colored flower pots, marble sprinkler basins, wrought iron resting benches and an indescribable abundance of everything that is civilization, leisure and fun. We could cry seeing all this and then looking at our torn short pants and worn heavy boots.

Nobody was in the streets yet. The guests were sleeping and only service personnel started opening the gates and cleaning the entrances. Naturally, we were rushed through these locations, so as not to be seen by anybody. Later, we realized that the probable reason for our very early alert was that we should pass this spa before its daily life started.

This procedure was repeated daily for months. The whole working day was spent in the border forest, where we had to cut the underbrush and young forest growths by the hundreds. We also had to fell trees and saw them into heavy trunk-discs, which were loaded in the afternoon onto peasant wagons. What bothered us the most was the work on *Shabbos* which was obligatory for everyone. We, the religious group, tried to minimize it as much as possible, but it couldn't be avoided completely since everyone had to finish a certain section of the forest.

Soon, I realized that we were counted only at marching out in the morning and at our return in the late afternoon. Whoever was present at the work place was assigned a section. I also noticed that as we entered Felixfurdo, there was a country house on the right side, where I saw religious Jews sitting in the afternoon. So, the next *Shabbos* morning, I slowly hung back from my line and started to fall back towards the last lines of our formation. Then, as we passed that Jewish house, I suddenly bent to the floor to fix my shoelaces while the other passed by. Then I jumped to the entrance gate and disappeared behind it as quickly as possible. No one reported me, and my detachment left.

In the yard, I was surrounded by the most friendly family I had ever met. They immediately told me to drop my tools in the corner and to come in for a rest and to hide. They were amazingly good and understanding. Later, it turned out that in their house there was a *minyan* for prayers, and I was invited for *Kiddush* and a meal fit for kings. I was just sorry for my comrades who were probably cutting branches on the mountainside.

I spent the most wonderful *Shabbos* afternoon in a long, long time, and in the late afternoon, at precisely the time they were marching back, I hid behind the gate and waited until they passed us. Then I slipped out and joined the last rows. Of course, it wasn't unnoticed anymore, and I later received a big reprimand from our Jewish detachment commander. I managed to convince him, however, that none of the army supervisors had noticed my disappearance. I offered him some material reward if he averted his eyes so that I could disappear from time to time and be free from the *Shabbos* work. He reluctantly agreed.

As time went on, I found out much information from the Jewish family in Felix, and slowly but surely a plan unfurled in my mind, waiting for the proper occasion to be carried out with the least possible risk. I decided to risk an unauthorized leave on a weekend to see my parents whom I hadn't seen for more than a year. No official leaves were granted to us anymore.

Everyone warned me that it was too risky and that I might wind up in a military jail or, at best, tied to a tree with my arms behind my back. Still, an irresistible urge drove me on to see my parents and to visit my beloved home after such a long absence. I waited for a long weekend combined with a holiday. The next possible chance was at the end of August, when the celebrations of St. Stephen's Day fell on a Monday, thus extending the weekend. I decided that this would be the occasion to try my luck.

I knew that under no circumstance could I trust my detachment leader with such a plan. The only ones in whom I confided were the family in Felix, because I needed their help. They also warned me of an additional danger, the border gendarmes, who were very strict and dangerously cruel. They constantly cruised Felix and the entire neighborhood, and anyone suspicious was likely to have a bitter encounter with them. I took this into consideration, but my daring was relentless. I didn't know why myself. It must have been a deeper intuition of my soul.

The family in Felix promised to lend me some civilian clothing and a hat, so that I should not look like somebody from the army. They were also supposed to buy train tickets from Felix to Nagyvarad and from there to Budapest. My express was supposed to leave at eight fifteen A.M. from Nagyvarad, and for this, I had to catch the first motor coach running out of Felix a few minutes after seven A.M. I chose Friday morning for my departure, to be able to spend a *Shabbos* with my parents. The express was supposed to arrive at two P.M. from Budapest, which would give me plenty of leeway so as not to travel on *Shabbos*.

On that morning, standing under the dark sky and waiting in line for coffee, I wasn't embittered. Rather, I was full of expectation as I looked at the myriad stars in the late August sky. Later, when we heard the first birds twittering at daybreak, I knew my sun was coming up and that this day wouldn't be another one of suffering. My close friends were puzzled at how I could be so happy before such a dangerous venture. In the dark forest, I started my plan, to retreat behind the lines and come to the end of the formation. Then, as we approached the part of the forest where dawn was already breaking, I silently stepped to the side of the road into the shadows. No one noticed me, and I overheard their usual stop before the underpass as they made their preparations to cross Felix. Presently, their voices became inaudible, and I was relieved. The first stage had gone smoothly. So far, so good.

I came all the way to the last tree and spotted the silhouette of the parked motor coaches. I hid in the last shadow, because I knew that on the other side of the embankment, the border police checked everyone entering the train. I saw their boots moving up and down along the tracks, and they presented the greatest danger for me, a member of the Hungarian army. After ten minutes, I became very nervous, because in the dark, I couldn't find the package of clothing which my friends promised to hide there for me. Finally, I found it hidden behind some trees further down the row. I quickly changed clothing and stuffed my work clothes into a bag, hiding it among the branches so that I could retrieve it on my way back.

I got as far as the embankment when I saw the shoes of the conductor mounting the steps of the motor car. There were only two minutes left to departure! I hastily climbed the embankment and waited behind a bush for the final trumpet of the conductor. The familiar blowing sounded, and the motor coach started rolling with a slight jolt. This was my chance. I stepped onto the outside stairs on the opposite side and held on to the black iron railing. The body of the coach shielded me from the gendarmes. A few minutes later, as we left Felix and were rolling through the open fields, I quickly opened the gate of the coach and entered the rear platform. The conductor was in the front and didn't notice me. I sat down between two other passengers who were only half awake, and by the time the conductor arrived, I had my tickets in my hands. He saluted with respect and left for the front. The motor coach speedily crossed the plains toward Nagyvarad, and I was on my way; my first temporary escape.

In the large railroad station of Nagyvarad, we had only ten minutes before the arrival of the express to Budapest. Luckily, I had my tickets in advance so I didn't have to go out into the big lobby where I could be seen by the gendarmes. I just switched tracks inside. The express was already packed by the time we got on, and it seemed I would have to stand in the aisles until Budapest, which wasn't a very appealing idea. Besides being tired, it wasn't to my advantage now to mingle with people. Then I recalled that my hosts in Felix had bought me a second-class ticket as a precaution. I couldn't bless them enough. The second-class compartments were almost abandoned, because they cost more. I felt like a "better" person as I slipped through the heavy glass door which had the golden Number Two on it, and I entered the plush, upholstered, exclusive compartment.

In the middle of the car, I found a completely empty compartment which I entered. I put my small package into the upper luggage holder and pulled the heavy curtains together.

It was cozy and exciting. I had not experienced such elegance since my teenage trips to the Tatras. I was pretty exhausted from the early morning adventures, and as the train started to roll out of the station, I gratefully ensconced myself into a corner, covered my face with the window curtain and fell asleep.

I don't know how long my deep slumber lasted. When I awoke, I realized I wasn't alone anymore. I heard men who had apparently lowered their voices so as not to awaken me. I picked up snatches of their conversation and realized they were talking in German, a language I knew from childhood. I decided not to move, because I was interested in what they were saying.

"*Pass auf was du sagst* (be careful what you say)," one of them warned.

"*Habe keine Angst, mein Freund der Kerl shlaft tief und wohl* (don't be afraid, my friend, the fellow is sleeping deeply and soundly)," was the self-confident answer.

Hearing this, my eyelashes almost vibrated, and slightly moaning as in a deep sleep, I changed positions, turning my head completely towards the corner so as not to show any reaction. The game started to be interesting. The two waited a few minutes to make sure I was still asleep and then started to talk without any hesitation in German.

"Yes, my friend, these stupid Hungarians think we don't see what they are doing. Their minister-president Kallay is openly undermining the policies of the Fuehrer. Since his speech in May, in which he openly refused the deportation of Jews from Hungary until their future fate would be outlined, everybody in the Reich knows that this man has to go. He will never cooperate with our Final Solution plans."

"I can tell you even more," the other man assured him. "I've just returned from Romania, where I was sent on a secret mission by the Federal Security Office. In Bucharest, I tracked down the covert activities of top Hungarian officers who, along with Romanians, are feeling out the English-American Allied Command in Turkey for possibilities of a separate cease-fire with the Russians. Do you realize what this would mean to us? The entire southeastern flank of our front would collapse. I am sure that when I report this back to Ribbentrop, very tough times will follow for these idiots. I hope Kallay and his government will be the first to be sent to the gas chambers. Let them pave the way for their Jewish proteges!"

It was a good thing that the train began violently shaking from a sudden brake movement, because I had to bite into the heavy curtain so as not to betray my excitement. I felt that by some mysterious Divine Providence I had fallen into the midst of a historic revelation. What a contrast! In the morning, I was still on the corner of my straw sack in the dark peasant room, hoping for my safe escape, and now I was speeding in a luxurious second-class express train and was overhearing a most dramatic conversation with regard to our future fate.

The sudden stop was for a construction zone, where the workers obediently pulled back to the sides of the tracks and were respectfully saluting the passing Oradea-Budapest express. When full speed was regained and they saw I still hadn't moved, they continued their conversation.

"I, for my part," boasted one of the men, "am laying the groundwork for the intervention of the *sonderkommando* (special commando forces). The SS wants to swarm into Budapest with full force as soon as the present government falls and we take over Hungary. Already, several lists have been drawn up by Berlin for possible new government figures. Of course, only the most radical German- sympathizing elements will be taken into consideration. Besides, they have to be real Jew-haters like Laszlo Endre and Baky.

"I guarantee you that if these guys come into power, they will outdo the SS High Command in killing Jews. They might even do the dirty work for us before any mass deportation is set in motion."

They started to laugh cynically and lit their cigarettes with contended pride.

"How much time do you give for the whole shake-up to take place?"

"Well, it depends greatly on what happens on the Russian front," said his partner, engrossed in his thoughts. "As I see it, I wouldn't give it more than next spring at the most. By that time, the Russians might be crossing the Carpathians, and then our High Command wouldn't play around with these stupid guys any more. Big actions will follow rapidly when Hitler will deem it the proper time for full intervention."

The blue cigarette clouds graciously floated all over the cabin.

"Watch your fumes, because it might wake up our fellow in that corner," warned the other.

This finally gave me the opportunity to change my stiff position without arousing any suspicion. Until now, I didn't dare move from fright. They might even kill me if they discovered I had overheard their secrets. The tension became unbearable. I gave a big sneeze, again and again, until I woke up moaning and stretching my cramped body. I looked around bewildered, making believe I didn't know where I was.

They smilingly looked at me as I called out in Hungarian, "Where am I now and who are you?"

They brought me up to date in broken Hungarian and assured me that I didn't have to worry, as there was plenty of time before our arrival in Budapest. I mumbled something and slowly regained my composure. I took the opportunity to leave the cabin and look for the rest room. I wanted to be alone with my thoughts and my anxiety. What should I do first? Should I alert all Hungary to such a tremendous danger? Thinking over the situation, I came to the conclusion that I couldn't do anything until I arrived at my parents' home and had taken up the entire matter with my immediate family.

I forced myself to look fully composed and went back to the cabin. I thanked them for letting me sleep so long, and together we opened the window to let the cigarette smoke dissipate. Then I started a very friendly conversation with them. They suddenly asked me if I knew or understood German.

"Oh, I wish I did," I answered with obvious consternation." I could use it so much in today's world. But I am so poor in languages. I am only good in geography and physics."

This declaration relieved them completely, and by the time the express reached the outskirts of Budapest and we started to get our packages ready, we were the best travel companions ever. This was the first big test of my life, and I had proved that I could retain my composure while anxious and tense inside. I think I passed the test, because we parted at the arrival platform with best wishes and "*auf wiedersehn.*"

I left the railroad terminal through a side entrance designed for service personnel and forbidden to passengers. I had to risk it rather than meeting any police or gendarme control, not to mention army intelligence officers. Soon I was outside on the well-known Thokoly Ut, and I flagged down the first taxi to speed me to my home where I hoped to surprise my dear parents and astonish them with the story of my adventure.

When I entered the old courtyard, it was a quiet afternoon hour. The dome-shaped doorway emitted that familiar pleasant coolness which I enjoyed so often in my younger years The maples peacefully nodded their foliage crowns. But I couldn't storm in unexpectedly on a Friday afternoon, without causing a shock to my parents and possibly also causing a commotion among the neighbors. I forced myself to return to the streets again. A half a block away, there was a public telephone booth. From there I called home. My mother thought I was calling long-distance, and she screamed in surprise at hearing my voice. She just didn't know what to talk about first. Then, cautiously, I brought her closer to the real situation, that I was not so far away, that I might be in the city and I might even be able to visit them. Finally, I came out with the truth, that I was just around the corner and had come for a visit for *Shabbos*. I then went to my father's workshop to give my mother a chance to get used to the sudden surprise. He was also shocked when I walked in and asked why I hadn't notified them of such a big event.

I called him into his inside office and told him I was on an unauthorized leave. He became quite nervous and abruptly directed his employees to pack everything and help him close the shop. I saw that his happiness upon seeing me was mixed with worry for my safety. He called a taxi, even though the distance home was short. He didn't want me to meet people on the streets. When I finally arrived home, my mother's welcome was quite different. She ran into my arms and kissed me with tears in her eyes, hugging and caressing me, trying to convince herself that it was really me.

My father remarked with a sad irony, "You see what a difference. Seems that your mother loves you more."

"I know exactly how you feel," I assured him. "You are just too afraid of the army discipline. But if you will hear my story, you will judge differently."

Thus, after the first surprise was over, we all started to prepare for the holy *Shabbos*.

Being in the company of my family around the *Shabbos* table, lit with sparkling candles and the smell of the fresh *Challah* on the table, was indescribably dear to me. We all felt that this occasion was something special. Who knew when it would be repeated, if ever?

After the meal, I revealed my entire story. I told them in advance that I considered the events I witnessed to be important for the Jewish public and maybe even for the whole country. Because of this, I was taking the liberty of talking about it at length even on *Shabbos*. Anyhow, my time was short, so I had to use every minute, no matter how much I would have enjoyed just sitting there and looking at my parents and sister and just being engulfed in the holy mood of *Shabbos*.

I told them how at first I had escaped, just out of an inner urge to see them. Then, by Divine Providence, I was a live witness to the most covert happenings. They were all amazed and disturbed. My mother was frightened, because she had already heard about the Nazi actions in Slovakia where her whole family was rounded up and taken to Poland in 1942. She foresaw the shadow of the same black horror overtaking our communities.

My father didn't take it so seriously. Maybe he only wanted to calm us down and set us at ease, but he declared that not everything could be taken at face value and that in Hungary a lot would have to happen in order to bring about such a radical turn of events. I wasn't quite of that opinion and told them I definitely wanted to do something about it.

My father asked me not to plan or decide anything on *Shabbos*, and he virtually forced me to wait at least until *Shabbos* ended. His wish forced a strained calmness upon us, but we felt he was right, and I didn't want to disturb their *Shabbos* anymore. After *Havdalah*, the real discussions and planning started. I told my father that I felt it my duty to alarm the entire Jewish community of the dangers facing them. And I felt it my duty to pass my information to the Hungarian government as well.

"My son, you don't realize what you did and how much trouble you are in now!" my father sharply retorted. "At present, you are a fugitive from the army and you are the least qualified person to present anything to any authority. No matter how great a service you would do them, they would never forgive you for leaving your unit without permission, and the first one to be put into jail would be you. At best, you are nonexistent here now. Be happy, if you can get back without any great difficulty."

I had to concede that he was right. Then he went a step further.

"Even if you would be clear and free now, counterintelligence would screen you a hundred times to see if the whole thing wasn't a fabrication on your part, and from what I know of their close ties with the Germans now, you might even wind up in the claws of the Gestapo. All of Budapest is full of double agents and traitors. You are much better off if you don't even start up with this news. Let them find it out through their own spies."

The soundness of my father's judgment was all too true. I felt the noose tightening around my neck, and I couldn't carry out a general alarm as I wanted to. Then I decided to stick to my real duty, to alarm my own people which I considered to be a *mitzvah* from the Torah. From that I wouldn't retreat.

My father couldn't object to this, but he anxiously warned me not to go public because I was not "legal" and if someone openly called the attention of the Jewish public to any general danger in these times, he would likely be labeled a scaremonger and panic spreader and might invite a lot of trouble for himself.

At this point, the overall caution of my dear father, who was really trying to protect me, gave me the feeling of being completely choked. I just couldn't take it anymore. For if I didn't act now, the danger to our people could not be averted. I could not worry about my own safety when Providence had entrusted me with the fate of thousands. On my insistence, on that same night, my father telephoned the president of the Orthodox Jewish National Council for a special meeting with his son early Sunday morning. It was quite difficult, and the appointment was only given after the secretary, a good friend of my father's, personally telephoned the president to say that a meeting of great public importance was to be convened. Again using a taxi, and leaving the house early, we were received by the president and his advisors in the office of the Orthodox Jewish National Council.

There, I openly told them in detail all I had heard and under what circumstances I had heard it. They listened to me carefully, but I didn't see the expected astonishment on the president's face nor on his advisors. They sat there like statues, maintaining their familiar frozen demeanor. As I finished and added that the entire Jewish community of Hungary was in imminent danger and that they should do everything in their power to help, I got a cool and somewhat reprimanding answer.

"Take it easy, young man," said the president. "We cannot just jump into hot water before it's even heated. Of course, what you just said is very useful, but we are aware of the fact that the Germans are constantly striving for tighter control and for a change of government. Kallay, the present minister, is a good man and a strong politician. He will not be easy to remove from his position, as even our regent is backing him."

My father was surprised that they were taking me, a young man, seriously enough to explain their position to me. But I wasn't so delighted. I desperately saw that they were minimizing the importance of my information.

"You want to tell me that all I heard wasn't enough for you to undertake positive steps to alarm our communities before it is too late?" I asked them straightforwardly.

The president's face melted into an ironic smile.

"Well, we are always closely watching developments around us," he answered. "And of course, when danger arises we will try to help as much as is in our power."

"If you wait until the danger arises it will be too late!" I burst out. "Your duty is to act while you can still prevent a tragedy!"

The president rose from his seat and raised his voice indignantly. "Our duty is our business, and you had better see to it that you get back to your army detachment quickly before you get into big trouble."

I became pale as the wall from such a covert threat. He is liable to denounce me to the police, I thought. My father grabbed my arm and asked them to forgive me for being so emotional. I didn't say a word and left the room without saying goodbye. I realized then why our people were doomed to perish all over Europe. The leaders were blind and haughty. They cared more for their own positions than for the safety of their brothers.

At home, a very heated family consultation followed. We were all very tense, because time was running out for my departure. It was already noon, and my express was supposed to head back to Oradea at four P.M. My parents kept looking at the clock, and my sister started to prepare food for my journey. This made me even angrier.

"Calm down!" My mother begged me. "You really did more than you should. The rest should be up to them. Soon, you have to make the train, and you must take a rest."

Hearing this, my suppressed fury exploded.

"You don't realize what's going on in the world, my dear parents!" I exclaimed. "You are living for the minute, as are thousands of others, and do not care that a tragedy in the making is about to befall you. Didn't you see what happened in Poland, Slovakia and Yugoslavia? Don't you know that almost all European Jewry has already been slaughtered? Do you still believe that by being peaceful and law abiding you are doing enough to protect your future? And the future of all of us?"

My hands were trembling, and my voice was piercing. They had to ask me not to be so loud lest the neighbors hear what was going on. I lowered my voice and told them that I had reached a new decision.

"I am not going back into the army," I announced. "I will go into hiding. I want to act, because those in the office will never do anything."

My father became noticeably pale. "You want to become an army deserter? Do you know what that means? Do you want to push yourself and your family into a tragedy?"

This confrontation with my father, whom I loved so much, was very painful to me. It hurt me that I had to excite him and that tears started to run down my mother's face.

"I'm so sorry for you," I continued sadly. "But you don't realize the gravity of the situation. Not only I but all of us will have to go into hiding. We have to make efforts to leave this country before it's too late. Never mind the Hungarian army now! Mind the life of our entire family and all the Jews. Why wait until they annihilate us, too?"

Seeing my determination, my father broke down completely.

"My son, you are now revolutionary, like every young man," he said. "But we are not prepared and not ripe for such ventures, and I guarantee you that none of our friends are either. No matter how darkly you paint their futures. I'm your father, and I have to save you from making a terrible mistake. As your father, I forbid you to do such a crazy thing now as to desert the army. You don't know what it means. I don't want you to fall into the claws of the army henchmen while the Hungarian army is at its full power yet. They would grind you to bits before you could do anything for Jewish survival."

Things became dark before my eyes. Here I was, in the middle of a family confrontation, and I had to choose between parental love and Torah-commanded obedience on the one hand, and between my moral duty to save lives. I had never had such a confrontation with my parents. Now, here I was with an explicit prohibition from my father and a dubious hope for any large scale help for my community. What should I do? Was I obligated to save or try to save my parents' lives against their own wishes? No one should have to face such a dilemma under such circumstances.

As I was standing there, inwardly fighting with myself,

looking at my father and glancing at my mother's tear-soaked face, my sister broke the tense silence and decided my plight. She pulled me over to the side.

"Don't press the issue now, and don't make them sick," she whispered into my ears. "Obey father now and wait for a better opportunity. This is not the proper moment for a decision against their will. Whatever you know now you'll know later, too, and you might be able to use it under less dangerous circumstances."

Her wisdom made me decide she was right, and I acceded to my father's wishes. With a deep sigh, I told them I needed to rest before taking the train back.

They kissed me with trembling hands, and my mother caressed my cheek for many minutes. We were all worn and pale, and we all took an hour's rest.

As the time approached for me to leave the house for the railroad station, to my surprise, they all declared that they wanted to accompany me to see me off. I was touched but felt a bit uncomfortable. Why this honor? But they insisted on coming.

Before I boarded the train, my father raised his hands above my head and blessed me, and my mother and sister kissed me again and again.

As I stood on the rear platform of the train and my family slowly receded into the distance, I saw them through my tears all waving goodbye. I had a very bad feeling, and I didn't know why this goodbye was more painful than any other. I had an urge to jump off the train and run back to them, because I had a feeling that something was wrong.

I returned to Felix with a broken heart and dead tired. My disappearance had been discovered, and the bad news awaited me that I would be hung with my arms tied behind me. Upon the night of my arrival, they put me into a makeshift jail and the sentence was to be carried out the next day.

That morning, however, our division got an urgent order

to pack up and return to headquarters at Nagyvarad at once. My sentence was suspended until we arrived at the army barracks, but it was never carried out because of the great changes taking place. I clearly felt that this was my reward for having obeyed my father.

I resumed my normal routine and kept serving the army with bitterness in my heart. I heard the words of my sister constantly in my ears and waited for the proper minute to act on my own. But I had missed my chance!

On March 19, 1944, Kallay barely saved his life by seeking refuge in the Turkish embassy. Horthy, the Regent, was forced to agree to a new Nazi-prescribed cabinet, and the arrest and deportation of the Hungarian Jews was immediately set in motion.

My mother sent me a desperate message that my father was beside himself, saying and repeating that I was right. I recalled the conversation of those German spies and sadly realized that being unprepared to act was a tragedy in itself. What could I have answered her? I asked her to be very calm and watch themselves and not to go out on the streets.

We forced laborers got an immediate Martial Law order that anyone escaping or even trying to escape would be shot on the spot. So my hands were tied, and I made no move until the mid-summer of 1944, when I deserted the army and went into hiding in Budapest. Only then did I find out that my parents had been sent to Auschwitz. I then understood why I had felt so terribly touched when my whole family waved goodbye to me at the railroad station. My innermost heart had known that it was the last time I would ever see them.

The Last Section of the Fence

■ ■ ■

Moshe Holczler

PESACH OF THE YEAR 1944 WAS ALREADY APPROACHING AMIDST
ominously threatening shadows. We all felt that our days were
numbered and that we were headed for disaster. Two weeks
after *Purim*, on March 19, 1944, the Nazis occupied Hungary,
and from that time on the biggest crime in Hungary was to be
a Jew. The virulently anti-Semitic Hungarian government
eagerly cooperated with the Nazi plans for our destruction,
and we all knew what was in store for us.

Immediately following the Nazi takeover, our forced labor
squadron put its units on alert. We boarded our cattle wagons
to cross the snow-clad King's Pass and headed down to
Nagyvarad. At that time, there were over thirty thousand very
fine Jewish families in the city, and we had hopes for the
possibility of spending *Pesach* there, perhaps to taste some
flavor of the *Seder* nights.

Arriving there, however, we were loaded onto army
trucks and taken to a small village on the outskirts. We were

placed in an old abandoned mill at the edge of town, under strict military surveillance. Our commander issued harsh orders and threatened sever punishments for the slightest violations of the rules of the enclosure. Our hopes faded fast. It took several days for us to find out that there was a small Jewish community in the town, but no contact was permitted. Later, we learned that when they wanted to offer kosher food for the religious boys of the squadron, they were refused outright by the commander.

"Even the skies darkened for us," we bitterly remarked, as the approaching days brought no relief.

"Seems like this year was not suited for a redemption . . . just like the other years," remarked one of our disillusioned comrades.

"Don't say that," retorted Rudy, an ardent believer. "*Pesach* is always *Pesach* and is a time for miracles for Jews. We should only be worthy of that!"

"You see what's going on," replied Ede. "One more week and we will sit on the straw sacks on the *Seder* night eating apples or raw potatoes for eight days."

The prospects were really very gloomy, and the general hostility around us indicated that this time Rudy would be wrong.

On the tenth day of *Nissan* of that year, a sudden change occurred. At the evening command assembly, after we marched in from work, there was an official call to "those elements who eat strictly kosher" to come forward and give their names. We were petrified! We were afraid to report, because we thought perhaps they wanted to punish us. After a repeated demand, topped with assurances not to be afraid, eight of us anxiously stepped forward. We knew the others would point us out in any case.

"So there are only eight out of two hundred and fifty," remarked the sergeant as he wrote down our names.

Then he told us that, at the fervent request of the local

Jewish community, we would be allowed to attend the two *Seder* nights at pre-arranged private homes. We would be taken there under military supervision and would be picked up the same way. We were told to wash and dress in our very best, so as not to bring shame to the unit.

Expressions of consternation and envy broke out on the faces of the rest of the boys. They had secretly hoped we were going to be punished, and now they pounded their fists in frustration and regret that they hadn't declared that they kept kosher.

And the miracle of *Pesach* happened again, even in that year!

There was a beautiful moon that night. Under the leadership of a corporal, we were marched in a festive column to the town. We arrived at the main plaza and were taken one by one to private homes where we were embraced by warm-hearted Jewish families. They were waiting for us as if this was the greatest reward they could possibly receive. We felt like we were in a dream; it was as if the angels of evil had lost their powers with the approach of the holiday, and the heavens had opened up. We saw that even the forces of destiny were powerless in these days, just as in ancient times in Egypt. I stayed with a lovely family with three small children, full of extraordinary warmth and affection.

Their little girl, with her curly blond hair, stole my heart when she jumped straight into my lap and didn't want to leave until she fell asleep. Those two nights were unforgettable and moving. With the deepest gratitude, we thanked our hosts and said goodbye after the second night. Loaded down with packages of *matzos*, eggs and meat, we returned to our quarters. Naturally, we distributed our *Pesach* food to everyone. For the first time, we were eyed with dignity and respect even by the non-religious.

A few days after *Pesach*, big loads of freshly cut timber were hauled in by Romanian peasants to the border of the town, and we learned that our new assignment would be to erect fences by digging holes and setting posts. We were surprised, because we had never done such work. We often cut undergrowth timber from those mountains, but we had never put up fences.

Some of the peasants were known to us. At the border, they would load the timber we cut on the donkey-drawn wagons, resenting this unpaid work for the Hungarian army. We found out from them that we were supposed to enclose the Jews of the town into a designated ghetto area.

We were outraged! Such cruelty! To force us to enclose our own brothers, the very ones who were so good to us, was a pure outrage! But our anger was to no avail. The order was given, and we were formed into groups and assigned sections. The barricade was to be erected in a matter of a few days.

I was so upset and ashamed that I sought an assignment away from my group, in order not to end up near the home of my *Seder* hosts. For two days I succeeded, but on the third day, my group commandant spotted me and ordered me back to my unit. I thought the world had caved in on me, knowing that we were headed towards that house.

A few days later, on a foggy, damp spring morning, we were commanded to the backyard of that friendly host's house, our picks, shovels and hatchets all laid out. We had just finished our black coffee when the sun's first rays hit the bedroom window. We saw hands nervously pulling at the curtains, but I also saw those curtains being lifted by small hands. Little heads soon peeped out, pushing their noses flat against the windows. I thought I would die of shame and turned away quickly so they shouldn't see my face.

Our scheduled work began, and by noontime, half the fence was standing behind their house. I tried to stand as far back as possible, handing things over to others rather than actually doing the work myself, but I was seething inside and suffering terribly.

When the noon break arrived, we sat down to eat beside the fence. All the boys were sad, but I almost couldn't eat. Suddenly, we heard the back door open and the footsteps of a child were running down the stairs.

The mother tried to catch up with her and yelled, "Don't go there, Malky. Come back here right away!"

I recognized the voice of my hostess, while at the same time I heard that the little steps didn't stop but were heading straight towards us. Soon, I recognized that lovely curly head running towards me with an excited face and wide open blue eyes.

She practically ran into me and burst out with anxiety, "Uncle, is it true that you are closing us in?" Her innocence couldn't accept the fact that this particular uncle, who was greeted so warmly by them, could do anything bad to them.

As I looked into those wide, disbelieving eyes, my eyes filled with tears. I caressed her blonde head and mumbled with remorse, "No darling, by no means. Some bad people want me to do it, but I wouldn't let that happen to you."

By this time, her mother arrived at the other side of the fence and indignantly put her head over the remaining opening.

"Malky, what did you do?" she scolded. "Are you not obeying?" Embarrassed, she turned to us while pulling her away from my lap. "Oh, I'm so sorry for this little devil."

Our eyes met, and saw that she understood my predicament. She didn't want to shame me.

I followed her a few steps, indicating that I wanted to tell her something.

"You can imagine how I feel about this, but I want to help you," I told her with a subdued voice. "Please tell your husband that before the fence closes I will sneak into your house. I want to talk to him."

She was amazed and grateful as she retreated with the child.

During the late afternoon break, I asked my comrade to cover for me while I slipped into the back cellar entrance, pretending to use the bathroom. My hosts waited anxiously while I hastily told them of my plan.

We all knew the ghetto was the first step to deportations. I would arrange with a Romanian peasant to take them up to the border forest where we got our timber. Once there, he would show them a little path which crosses over into Romania. I discovered this path when I was sent for water while working up there. Finding a spring, I also found myself surrounded by Romanian border patrols, who allowed me to take water and return to Hungary. I wanted to use this little discovery to the advantage of my hosts. I told them to be ready very early, before daybreak, when the peasants set out for their journeys and the gendarmes are not yet around. They asked for time to think it over and promised to give me an answer the next day to my work-site.

During that night, I couldn't sleep. "What a crazy and dangerous thing you arranged!" my comrades badgered me.

"I just couldn't face that curly blond head with her wide open blue eyes," I kept mumbling, my hands clenched into fists. "We are just no good if they can make us jail our own hosts."

In the meantime, I had already spoken with my Romanian peasant who, after some hesitation, agreed to hide them among some feed which he took up to his field on the mountainside. For a sizable amount of money, he would eventually lead them over to Romania. I was now concerned whether they would be mature enough to size up their own situation and decide to follow my advice.

The next day, we moved on to the next property with our fencing job. Only two sections were still open on the entire ghetto fence, of which one would be finished today. If my hosts were not gone by the next day, there would be no more chance to escape.

At noon, I again dashed into their basement and called their attention to the situation. To my satisfaction, they had already decided to accept my offer. They discovered a relative living in Tenke, the next town in Romania, which was about twenty kilometers from the border. At least, they had somewhere to go in a strange country. No deportations were allowed in Romania, though there were sporadic outbursts of anti-Semitic hatred.

In the late afternoon, before marching back, I again met them behind the fence and gave them their final instructions from their pre-dawn departure. I said goodbye. They were supposed to wait at the last open section of the fence to be picked up by the Romanian peasant whose name was Miculescu. There were tears in my eyes as I offered them my best wishes in answer to their gratitude for my rescue venture. The little girl again found her way into my arms for a goodby kiss, and I promised to visit her some time in the future.

The next morning when I arrived at work to close up the last section of the gate, they were already on the mountain path which led them through the Romanian border to safety.

The Germans Invade

■ ■ ■

Sarah Holczler

IT WAS FRIDAY, MARCH 17, 1944. IN OUR FAMILY, IT WAS HIGHLY
unusual to travel on *Erev Shabbos*, but I was anxious to go to
my sister's home in Budapest, for I had heard that my *chasan's*
work brigade was somewhere near there. If only we could
meet! He had recently sent news that they expected to be
moved towards the frontier, perhaps to the Ukraine.

The war's dark clouds gathered over our heads. Hardly any
families included fathers and older brothers anymore. With
the grown men missing, the authorities began calling in young
boys.

I can still feel my father's disapproval of my decision to
travel on Friday. Saying goodbye to him, I bent down to kiss
his hand, an old family custom, but he pulled his hands away.

I took the early morning train, travelling three to four
hours, and arrived at my sister's home hours before *Shabbos*.
There, a desperate message from my *chasan* awaited me. His
unit had been denied furlough. We would not be able to meet.

Shabbos was very quiet and foreboding.

On Sunday morning, March 19, I took a tramcar and travelled to Buda to visit my elderly aunt, who lived there in an old-age home. Her husband had been a *mashgiach* (religious supervisor) for the Orthodox Congregation, and as his widow, she was entitled to this nice, well-kept retirement home.

Alighting from the tramcar, I hurried up the steps leading to the home. A curious sight caught my eye. There were long rows of military compounds nearby. With their open windows now housing machine gun units facing the street, they resembled porcupine needles sticking out towards us and the street. The effect was very strange and frightening.

I reached the top of the steps when a man rushing down towards me, hissed urgently in passing, "The Germans are here! Run home!" I recognized the man as one of the doctors from a nearby Jewish hospital. My heart nearly stopped in terror! I turned and ran to the nearest tram station, all the while whispering to myself, "I must get home! Oh, why didn't I listen to my father's admonition?"

Most of Hungary's Jews were sure their fate would not be the same as that of the Jews in other countries. After all, our nation was friendly with the Germans, comrades-in-arms, fighting together on the Russian front. Our Jewish sons were in working brigades helping the Germans.

I, however, never held the same illusions. While many of my friends got engaged and even married during that dreadful time when we were stripped of our livelihoods by the infamous anti-Jewish laws, I could not sleep from worry. I started to plan escape routes for my parents. I obtained false gentile identification papers from our servant. I bought a toy gun and a bicycle, thinking they would come in handy if I had to run from the German's. I was never naive.

In 1942, I befriended a noble, young Christian woman and her eight-year-old son, who came from a titled family in

Transylvania. Her first husband hated the Germans and had been killed by them. She had subsequently married a drunkard. Her sole financial support came from me. Somehow, I had prepared for her a special role should the need ever arise; she would hide my parents.

All of these thoughts tumbled and twirled through my feverish mind on that long tramcar ride. On the banks of the Danube River, I saw the ominous, long, gray snaking lines of moving German hardware; tanks and army trucks were moving unopposed, covering the entire horizon. With tearful eyes, I saw our destiny shaping up as in my worst dreams.

Arriving back at my sister's house, I saw that the dreadful news had preceded me. Desperation was everywhere! My brother-in-law huddled together with some of his friends, feverishly planning an escape for his family and giving advice to them.

I had but one desire—to get home! Two of my cousins who were from the same town were in the city, and I wanted to speak with them. Although we hardly dared step into the street, I sneaked out anyway. Looking over my shoulder for Nazis every second, I finally got to my cousins. They were as determined as was I to get home. We agreed to take an early train from the main terminal, the Keleti, the next day.

That night, about three o'clock in the morning, I heard my sister's bedroom door open. Knowing I probably couldn't sleep, she rushed to my bedside, glancing at my suitcase, packed and ready for departure.

"I can't let you go!" she began to cry. "I can't let you go! I will never see you again. I cannot lose my only sister. Please! I had a premonition that you will never make it home. They will take you!"

She took me, pleaded with me and even threatened me, but I would not allow her to weaken my determination to go home and try to save my parents. I knew they would never have the courage to hide by themselves.

The sun, the horrible sun, broke through the grayish clouds, and the daylight filtered through the curtains and found us sobbing in each other's arms.

Time for departure came and went without me. I grudgingly remained with my sister for a few days more. When the news came from home that both my cousins failed to arrive home after taking the appointed train ride I was supposed to take with them, I felt the special *hashgachah* of my sister's premonition.

Later, we learned that the first victims to arrive in Auschwitz were Jews gathered from the train and bus stations, as everybody's first impulse had been to be together with their families. The Germans knew this from previous experience.

So we embarked upon a new emergency plan, to send *shlichim* (paid agents) to bring our parents to Budapest. We felt that, in a big city, there were always more possibilities to hide since my parents were unknown persons.

However, we did not take into account that my wonderful father, whose whole life was occupied with *mitzvos* and *maasim tovim,* would be arrested by the Hungarian gendarmes as a leading citizen and taken at midnight for a "confession" to the dreaded Nazi terror base. He had been singled out because of a report from a hostile Christian neighbor who was envious of our material well-being.

We learned this terrible news through the noble Christian woman whom I had befriended. She had sent her only child to sneak into the ghetto at night to deliver our letter to our mother and collect hers to send us.

We knew that time was very short to perform some miraculous saving act and notified our mother that a young man would sneak her out of the ghetto. We implored her to be ready at the appointed time, but she would not leave my father. Aside from that, she was too broken and terrified to act, even though all the details had been worked out.

The last report came from this heroic young man (a

disguised Jew) who last saw our mother between two para-
troopers, carrying a lunch pail to our father in prison. She
realized who the man was, and she signaled a barely percep-
tible "No."

My father miraculously survived the brutal beatings,
"confessing" to everything his tormentors demanded, giving
away whatever was hidden. Then he was tossed, broken, back
into the ghetto a short time before the Jews there were herded
into cattle cars and taken to Auschwitz.

His last heroic act was to carry an empty pail, before he
was pushed into a cattle car, and implore the jeering, gaping,
happy onlookers for a little water to take along for the babies.
One of the murderous gentiles tore it from his hands and kept
it. The onlookers were old-timers with whom my father had
grown up in the same town.

And I was destined to live!

We all went into hiding. Very shortly afterwards, I received news that my *chasan* had unexpectedly "taken" a
furlough, due to the political turmoil in the army, and risking
his life, he had hurried to Budapest to seek me out.

We arranged an emergency wedding in a "yellow star"
house before the curfew. The condemned Jews were prohib-
ited from marrying at that time and were threatened with
immediate death. My only sister came out of hiding to be
present. The courageous rabbi was an old friend of the family.
The *Chuppah* was held in a shaded room with a *tallis* as a
canopy. The bridal veil was a borrowed cap and my cape was
a borrowed sweater. Ten pale, trembling Jews, all strangers,
stood as witnesses. We were unexpectedly treated to chicken
soup by a relative. It was our delicious wedding feast!

Then, we slipped out of the ghetto. My husband to his
unit, and I to my hiding place.

A Mission of Rescue

■ ■ ■

Sarah Holczler

I RECEIVED AN OMINOUS LETTER FROM MY HUSBAND THROUGH a secret channel telling me that within a few short days they would be transported to the Ukraine from their base in Szeged. The letter contained an urgent plea to help him escape.

My heart skipped a beat as I looked around the sunny, comfortable apartment in the heart of Buda. It was the safe haven of Ilona Raday, a middle-aged, unmarried gentile woman. She introduced me as her cousin from Transylvania, a well-established Aryan. For this she received an enormous amount of money, which came to her as a monthly payment from my brother-in-law.

That night, when she came home from one of her numerous parties, she was slightly tipsy from drinking. Lurching towards me, she tried to focus her bleary eyes while listening to my problems.

"You're not normal!" she exclaimed. "You want to throw

away your own life for a man? So what if he is your husband? Surely, you will be arrested the moment you leave my house."

My husband wrote to me that according to his plan, I was to arrive in Szeged where his work brigade was stationed at a brickyard. He had befriended the watchman's family, whose daughter would wait for me at the train station. He told them that Katalin Kovacs (the name I assumed), an Aryan girl, was his wife, and he wanted to see me before he was deported elsewhere. The watchman of the brickyard lived in the center of the compound in a small house, and in exchange for a gift, they had agreed to accept me as an overnight guest. I was to bring along invisible ink, money and my own credentials.

After much persuasion, I got a firm promise from Ilona Raday that she would accompany me to the dreaded main railroad station in Budapest, the Keleti Station. This junction was the most heavily guarded by the Nazis. They maintained a constant vigil there to catch escaping Jews.

The morning of my departure came. I said my prayers, my battered valise ready. My faded gingham dress and worn shoes attested to my changed personality. I was Katalin Kovacs, of gypsy origin, and a housemaid. In the next room, the walls were vibrating from the heavy snoring of my patron. In vain, I tried to wake her into sensibility. She opened one eye when I tried to remind her of her promise to accompany me to the station.

"You stupid Jewess!" she shouted. "Go, throw your life away. What do I care? Let me sleep!"

That desperate sense of isolation set me free. Life did not seem precious anymore since our parent's deportation, at least not my life. I just wanted to save my husband's life.

Still, I dreaded falling into Nazi hands. There was no way out. I had to go through the main station at Keleti. In the morning stillness, I could only hear occasional hammering, as the Jewish stars were nailed to the gates of the designated Jewish houses. After uttering a soft *Shema Yisrael*, I entered the station and bought my ticket to Szeged. There was hardly any activity, it being a Sunday morning. A few Hungarian storm troopers were hanging around. The scene was quieter than I had expected. I got on the train, and, oh what a relief, it started to roll.

There were other passengers on the train, mostly workers, peasants and one gypsy woman. I tried to look and behave like one of them. After a while, we pulled into a station. Before our eyes, we saw long rows of cattle cars stationed there, and my heart skipped a beat. Jews were being herded into them. They came in endlessly long rows from the direction of the town, old worn faces, frightened, bent shoulders, some on crutches, women pushing baby carriages. I cannot forget one young girl who was standing a little bit to the side looking as if some interesting adventures lay ahead. She looked like a country girl, and in her face there was an innocence only a young girl could show.

All the passengers in my compartment jumped up at the sight and were fighting and pushing to get to the window for the best place to see. They were laughing and became very happily excited.

"Oh, how good!"

"They are taking all the dirty Jews!"

"I hope they kill all of them!"

Suddenly, one of them turned to me. "Miss, come and see this wonderful sight."

I was standing among them, but I wasn't fighting for the best view. I was praying inwardly that I should be able to bear the sight without my heart breaking aloud. My face turned to stone.

All of a sudden, a piercing scream was heard. "The Lord will punish you! He will wipe you off the face of this earth! Innocent people are murdered and you dare to laugh and revel in the pleasure of it!"

I could not believe my ears. The gypsy woman was

screaming. Her eyes were rolling, she tore up her blouse and she beat her breast with her fist as tears ran down her wrinkled face. All the while, she was screaming, "The Lord will punish you horribly!"

This open defiance of that cruel, inhuman laughter was so shocking, that for a moment there was not a sound. How I wanted to run to her, embrace her, and cry with her.

The silence did not last long. The crowd got over their surprise, and the sudden fury of their reaction set in.

"You dirty gypsy!" they shouted. "You feel with the Jews? We will throw you to the dogs, too. If you don't shut up we will call for help to remove you, and you will join the Jews."

The gypsy woman, completely spent, withdrew into her corner, and the train finally pulled away toward Szeged.

It was early afternoon when I arrived in Szeged. I got off the train and looked around to find the girl, who according to our plan, was supposed to wait for me. I noticed a plain-looking girl in her late twenties coming towards me.

"Are you Katalin Kovacs?" she asked me.

"Yes," I answered.

"Well, your husband asked me to meet you, and he gave me your picture so that I should be able to recognize you. Let's get out of here. I have some bad news to tell you."

As we walked, she said, "Until this morning the working brigade was stationed in the brickyard. It was a quiet place and you could have met your husband without any difficulty. However, this morning an urgent order came, and the whole unit (many hundreds of the Jewish working brigade) had to evacuate the brickyard in a hurry, because they are bringing in all the Jews from the town and vicinity. Your husband told me you should stay with us and in the evening he will try to come and visit you."

When we arrived, the brickyard looked very dreary and deserted. In the middle of the yard there was a tiny watchman's hut. My heart sank at the desolate prospect. The girl's parents received me quite cordially but with obvious apprehension. They explained that the situation had changed drastically and they themselves might be evacuated. They had no idea where those poor boys were stationed now. They pitied me greatly because I had bound myself to a Jewish boy at such a terrible time.

Dusk was approaching. They half-heartedly invited me for a meager supper. I declined and took out my sandwich, explaining that the stress I was under took away my appetite. As I looked through the tiny window, hoping for some messenger to bring word of my husband, I saw many army trucks arrive at the gate. Storm troopers poured out of them. The loud commands of the sergeants were heard as they ordered the troops to form a human chain around the compound.

The air froze in the tiny hut. My host began wringing his hands.

"Oh, miss!' he lamented. "This portends great danger. Your husband doesn't know what is happening here. He will come tonight, and we will all end up in jail."

Scarcely an hour had passed in this anxiety-ridden atmosphere when the big gate was again thrown open and the first Jews arrived. They came in long columns, weary, panic-stricken, elderly people with fear in their eyes. They carried their bags on their bent shoulders, the eternal "wandering Jews." Women with baby carriages, young girls, children streamed through. There was a shrill mixture of human sound and the dissonant wails of suffering. Storm troopers, yelling gruffly, ordered the downtrodden Jews in all directions, lashing out at them with fists and rifle butts as the terrified mothers tried to keep their children close to them. They were so close to us, we could see every dusty wrinkle on their agonized faces. The children cried for a little water. All this I witnessed through the window. As a Jew, I had to suppress my anguish at the indescribable cruelty and jeering of the storm troopers.

Somehow, nightfall brought a measure of tranquility. Only the babies' cries and the whispering voices of the mothers could be heard from the distance.

Renewed anxiety about my husband overcame me. It grew with each hour to an unbearable pitch of tension as the neighborhood dogs started to bark. With each bark, my heart skipped a beat.

"Maybe they are barking because my husband is trying to get in," I thought. "He doesn't know what's in store for him."

In utter desperation, I suggested to Margit, the daughter, that we sit outside on the bench since we couldn't fall asleep. I desperately wanted to intercept my husband in case he arrived. She gladly consented, and we sat down.

In the near distance, behind wooden planks, I could hear the crying, moaning and whispering by the crowded Jewish masses. They were occasionally interrupted by the harsh, cruel bellowing of the jailkeepers. There were many suicidal moments when I wanted to cry out in unbearable heartache and join my people.

Just when such a desire took my breath away, a couple of troopers unexpectedly discovered us in the darkness and playfully joined us.

"Nice evening, isn't it?" they said. "All the Jew animals rounded up for the slaughterhouse. Come, let us sing."

Margit joined half-heartedly as I was prodded to join in. Somehow, I felt the *hashgachah* that maybe if I would talk and get on friendly terms, they could help me with my husband if he came. So we sat and talked, singing occasionally, which was the natural thing to do. Behind us, my people were crying and dogs were barking. Every bark made me shudder and think my husband was approaching.

I overheard one trooper, a singularly evil-looking man, ask Margit who I was. She said I was a cousin who was just visiting. I don't know how much time went by, the weariness, fear and constant watchfulness, having dulled my senses. My escort asked me for a date. He suggested a movie the next afternoon. I consented and made a definite date. Suddenly, a sharp, powerful flashlight blinded me as it was cruelly focused into my eyes.

"Let me see you!" a rough voice said. "Aha! I thought so. You look suspicious to me!"

As tears ran down my face from the persistent, blinding glare, my escort jumped up and indignantly protested such treatment of "his" girl. They must have been from the same village, because my escort called him by his first name. However, the man was of higher rank. Finally, he relented and when my eyes got used to the darkness again, I saw his cruel face staring at me. He reluctantly yielded and started to go, threatening that he would take care of me. I tried to shrug off the incident, and my escort did so too, with a barely audible mutter that the man was a very dangerous fellow, indeed.

We bade each other goodnight, promising not to forget our movie date.

I was more dead than alive when we finally turned into our beds. I was already a little bit relieved about my husband, reasoning that if he had not yet arrived, he would not come so late at night. As I tried to catch some sleep, I saw the pale sky breaking into daylight. When at last, all the disturbing sounds around us became fainter, I slipped into a slumber.

The next morning, I looked through the window and saw more Hungarian storm troopers converging with bayonets fixed. They gave loud orders and cursed all the Jews who did not know how to die quietly. One of them, just beneath our window, remarked, "I wish I could shoot them all right here and be finished with these cockroaches!"

The hatred was so virulent, it came so much from their hearts, that no matter how history will try to whitewash them, saying that they did it under German orders, their guilt will never be erased. The Hungarians were born anti-Semites, ready and willing at any moment to kill Jews.

The door opened, and Margit's mother came in.

"Please, miss," she said. "Do not mind what I have to tell you, but we did not foresee what would happen here. My husband is very worried about you. There was another inquiry about you this morning, and we were questioned at length about you. We do not think it safe for you to stay here any longer. I truly hope you can still get out, but it would be advisable to go as soon as possible."

My heart contracted with fear. These words reinforced what I was feeling inside, but to hear it from this plain woman was a clear-cut threat. I gulped down my black coffee and took my valise. With a word of thanks, I said goodbye to them.

Outside, I tried to calm my heart, and lightly singing to myself, I leisurely strolled towards the gate. It was frightening to see the awesome fortifications erected during the night against this innocent population, mostly old people, women and children. They put up barbed wire and constantly reinforced the guards. It was a disgrace, the precautions taken, as if those powerless captives were a serious enemy threat.

When I had almost reached the gate, a loud, rough voice shouted after me, "Stop, or I'll shoot you!"

I stopped immediately and turned around. The very same devil of the previous night was rushing towards me with such fury, his face flushed with anger, that I instinctively backed away.

"What is the matter with you?" I screamed, scarcely concealing my fear. "Are you out of your mind?"

"You will be out of your mind when I arrest you," he replied.

"Oh, and on what basis, dear sergeant?" I said.

Before he could answer me, all the while his gun pointing at my heart, my escort of the previous night came running out of somewhere.

"You miserable cur," he shouted. "What do you want from my girl?"

"How do you address me, you nobody?" the devil answered. "I will finish you off with your Jewess together!"

He suddenly turned his gun towards my escort, causing him to rush towards him with his fist.

"What did you call my girl?" he retorted in a rage.

They started to fight with fists, kicking and hitting each other, and I grabbed my suitcase and I flew out the gate, away from this hellhole.

I ran until I was out of breath, then after making a turn, when I felt hidden from that gate, I forced myself to calm down. I didn't want to be conspicuous on the sunlit, almost deserted street.

As I strolled, outwardly calm, and the black circles in front of my eyes started to fade, an endlessly long road stretched before me. Somewhere at the end I saw a little black spot which started to grow. I thought my eyes were still clouded, but those black spots kept growing, and to my dismay, took up human form. It was undoubtedly another human column, beating up the dust, approaching the center of the road.

In a panic, I wanted to escape, but there was nowhere to go. Both sides of the street were enclosed with houses and there was no open gate. I had to continue and brace myself for the oncoming long rows of Jewish people. As I now openly faced them, I had to be careful not to show any emotion or appear as a fugitive. They came slowly, with hunched shoulders, old men, women with baby carriages, dust-wrinkled young faces, carrying their meager worldly possessions of one bag each. Every ten yards, on both sides, were storm troopers with fixed bayonets.

I tried to keep my eyes straight ahead on the sidewalk, so as not to see them, hoping they would not see me. When I reached the middle of the walking column, a young girl with frightened, protruding eyes suddenly shouted out my Jewish name, "Szori!"

I saw the nearest storm trooper grab the bayonet as he

suddenly turned to me. He was so close, I could see his piercing eyes. I felt a crushing roar in my ears, my eyes clouded, my heart stood still . . . but my legs mechanically continued to carry me forward. And the column passed me.

For years, those terrified young eyes haunted me, reflecting that young confused mind, who upon seeing me alone felt I was in danger. I could not remember who she was. The mystery was solved only years later by my cousin who survived the concentration camp and to whom this girl poured out her anguish at the thought that she had surely sent me to the death camp on account of her foolishness.

As I was heading for nowhere, weakened to the utmost from the shocking experiences of the day which had just barely begun, I did not know where to go. Where would I find my husband . . . if I could find him at all? I no longer had any place to stay. The only clue I had was that they were ordered in these days to clean the debris after the air raids. But who knew where those places were?

I was standing at a crossroad, fervently wishing I could hide my valise some place, not to show my transitory position, which was such a giveaway in a city filled with deported Jews. I saw another column of people approaching. This time, it was the Jewish working brigade. I tried to look at them, hoping for some clue about my husband, when I noticed that one of the men grabbed someone's arm and motioned towards me. The other man turned around. It was my husband!

Oh, how I felt the *hashgachah* from above for the great miracle of seeing my husband again! I no longer felt all alone. It was such a relief; all the terror I had felt before faded from the slate of my memory.

I tried not to be too conspicuous, but all I could do was follow the troops from a distance so that I shouldn't lose sight of them again. After a few city blocks, I saw the working brigade come to a halt as they unloaded their heavy tools, spades and pickaxes and started to dig in the debris.

With my new-found strength and confidence, I lingered nearby, using all kinds of stalling tactics like searching for my handkerchief and powdering my nose. In my naivete, I thought that only my husband and his closest comrades would notice me. I hoped and prayed that my actions would not cause him any harm. To my happy surprise I saw my husband purposefully crossing the street towards me. He urgently whispered an order telling me to go into a nearby roofless, half-demolished building and then ran back to his unit.

It was heaven behind those all-embracing, cool walls, away from human eyes. For a few minutes their protectiveness gave me a home-like feeling. As if to emphasize the normalcy of the surroundings, a nearby church's bells started to chime, signalling that it was noontime. I imagined the citizens sitting down to their well-accustomed continental midday meal, comfortably munching their food, without a thought about the suffering of the unfortunate Jewish masses with a death threat hanging over their heads. Then my husband appeared.

His face was lined with white dust, his skin dark, but his happy smile nullified all my observations. He explained the special *hashgachah* of today. Their sergeant was ordered to the deportation camp, and a Jewish leader was assigned to take the unit out here to clean up the debris until the sergeant returned. He was expected back in about half an hour.

I quickly told him about the night, the morning and my impending "date" with the soldier. He experienced agony over last night's failure to meet me. Fortunately, he called the watchman's house on the phone, and when he heard the rough military voice, he understood that the place was occupied by storm troopers. Without identifying himself, he put down the receiver.

The Jewish brigade leader who gave us permission for these precious few minutes of freedom (after my husband briefed him about our situation) advised him, after appraising my courage and the danger we were in, that I should go to the unit officer, a colonel, and try to beg for a day off. It was a daring and unusual request but not impossible being that I was a "gentile" woman married to a Jew. However, by no means should I try to come after them anymore.

My husband then explained the location of the military compound and assured me of his fervent prayer for me. In case my request would not be granted, I should purchase a suit and hat with accessories and try to sneak out here again. He was determined to escape, because according to an announcement made by the unit officer, the unit was preparing to leave for the Ukraine. My husband encouraged me, assured me that Hashem would help me stay out of trouble. After all, this was the *mitzvah* of *pikuach nefesh* (saving a life). With a heavy heart, we said goodbye, and he left.

I stayed a little while and tried to summon my faltering courage. It was so good to sit in the shade, behind protective walls, and I wanted to postpone that horribly dangerous mission.

Finally, I collected myself, regaining my shaky confidence. After all, I was doing it to save my husband's life! I stepped into the boiling hot, sunny street. I hurried away from the working brigade and went in the direction of the business district. I was searching for a hotel. I did not have to walk far when I saw a hotel sign. The streets, due to the noon meal, were deserted.

I stepped into the foyer of an old fashioned hotel. It was cool and dark inside. When my eyes adjusted to the dimness, I saw a sleepy-eyed clerk perched behind a counter.

"I need a room," I said.

"For how long?" he questioned me.

"Oh, a couple of days," I answered.

He looked at my worn-out luggage doubtfully. "You have to pay a day in advance and fill out this application form."

After the preliminaries, he took me upstairs to a dark, narrow room facing another room, divided by a skylight. I couldn't voice any objections. After all, who was I? A maid of "gypsy" origin!

My first movement was to pull the shades down and use the sole electric bulb for light. It was a dark, unfriendly room. It gave me the shivers. Instead of feeling a little bit relieved to be away from the streets and within protective walls, I suddenly felt trapped in a dangerous cage.

Originally, I planned to lay down and rest a little bit, because I was tired and spent, but in this room there was no peace, only a chilling uneasiness. I refreshed myself and realized with a jolt how short my time was until my promised date with the soldier and my impending mission with the head of the army unit. I felt I should already be on my way to my husband's unit and at all costs avoid meeting the soldier on the street.

I searched my suitcase (which I wanted to leave behind) for any telltale sign, fully expecting the clerk to pry into its contents.

Downstairs, the clerk looked up with surprise. "Are you leaving so soon?"

"I have a date with my sergeant boyfriend," I answered lightly, "but I'll be back."

He stared dubiously at my faded gingham dress, and I could feel the doubt creeping into his eyes as he looked me over. Somehow, my fine manners were not in accord with my occupation. To avoid any further scrutiny, I asked for a duplicate key and hurried out.

My stomach started to rumble, I was so famished. To my relief, I saw an old woman squatting next to a basket of apples on the next street corner. I bought a bagful of delicious apples and started to eat on the way. (This was in conformity with my outfit.)

Impatience drove me towards my goal, and somehow, hurrying on the streets made me feel safer to be on the move.

After a few inquiries and a long walk, I arrived at the

forbidding army headquarters building. After saying a quiet *Shema Yisrael*, I entered the gate at the main entrance. A soldier with a bayonet in hand asked me for identification. I handed it over with a straight face. He scrutinized it with a stupid expression, reading it half aloud, as an illiterate would do, and sent me upstairs. My body never felt so heavy in my life as I managed to climb up the marble steps. I felt I was nearing a deathtrap.

Upon arriving at the door, another soldier with a bayonet asked for my credentials and asked me at length the reason for my visit. This soldier was more intelligent. He finally relented and opened the door to the colonel.

To my relief, he was a kind-faced, middle-aged intellectual. He motioned me closer and looked at me inquiringly. As simply as possible, I explained that I was married to a Jewish man. We were married only a few months, and now I had come to see him before he was taken further away. All I wanted was a day or half a day off to be together with him. Who knew what the future would bring? Would the colonel kindly grant this humanitarian request?

He looked at me sadly and told me I had chosen the worst possible time for my request. They were constantly on "alert," and any time off from the garrison would be impossible.

"You really tied your fate to a Jew at the worst possible time," he added rather warningly. "I would advise you to save your life and sever your ties with him for the time being. Do not fall into the sad fate that awaits them."

He dismissed me quite abruptly. There was nothing else to do but leave. I was sad and immensely relieved at the same time. The ordeal was over, and I had survived it with Hashem's help. But what about the future?

Now that I had survived the interview with the army colonel, I had to worry about where to shop for my husband's civilian outfit. How much easier it would have been to talk things over with him, but all the further planning was left entirely to me. The only comforting thought was that I had ample money due to the generosity of my sister who had insisted I take a lot with me. How I blessed her for it now!

I found the shopping center and went to a men's clothing shop where I bought a simple suit, a hunter's hat and accessories. In the meantime, I tried to shop far away from any movie theater, because I dreaded encountering the storm trooper, as the time for our date was dangerously approaching. Again, I headed towards the bombed-out section of the city where they worked, hoping our luck would hold and that somehow I would find my husband and give him the civilian outfit I had bought for him. Now I was really apprehensive lest anyone catch me doing my suspicious shopping, but I was determined to prevail. Hashem would continue to help.

I strolled again among the bombed-out houses. I feared my husband would be punished by the troop leader if he approached me. But my luck held out. His friends covered for him, and he motioned me to come over to him quickly. I crossed the hot, dusty road, and he made me squat down behind an open wall. I told him of my failure to obtain a short furlough from the commander and of going shopping for the necessities. He quickly hid the package beneath large stones and told me to keep the hat for him.

He gave me his university certificate and instructed me to alter the letters to a gentile name with the invisible ink I had brought along from Szeged. He explained how to use the invisible ink. The first application had to be completely dry. Then, when the old writing disappeared, the new lettering could be written over it.

He asked me to go immediately and buy two tickets to Budapest for the train leaving at midnight. Again he assured me that his fervent prayer would accompany me on my dangerous mission. He planned to escape that night, for tomorrow his unit would be dispatched to the Ukraine.

We agreed that with Hashem's help we would meet at

eight o'clock two blocks before the train station on a certain street if everything went well with his daring plan. His only identification papers were placed in my hands. We said a quick goodbye with prayers on our lips.

I left with a terribly heavy heart. It seemed to me that the whole weight of our survival was on my shoulders. The fear for my own safety was overshadowed by this tremendous responsibility.

I said some prayer and headed towards the dreaded railroad station, a potentially dangerous place which was usually cordoned off by the state troopers. I was expecting the worst as the entire flow of deportation passed through this station.

The special *hashgachah* which accompanied us thus far was again hovering above me. The station was rather deserted (a group had probably just left), and I purchased two one-way tickets to Budapest without a hitch. Having the little paper tickets in my possession made such a big difference. I already felt more secure and relieved.

The gnawing hunger in my stomach reminded me that I had only eaten a few apples a whole day. In the hotel room there was a sign which said no eating was permitted in the rooms, so I bought a few rolls and apples and placed them in my bag to take to my hotel room.

When I arrived at my hotel, the clerk received me with a stern face.

"The police were just here to question me about our registered guests," he said. "I told them you just left a while ago but would be back. So be ready in case they come back soon."

"I have very little time left, because I have a date," I said. "Do you think I cannot leave when I have to? Do I have to wait for them?"

"Well, that's up to you, but if you have nothing to fear you can leave when you want to."

I went up with cold shivering hands and got my belongings together. Then I remembered my husband's identification paper and the ink. I had no alternative but to do it right away. I pulled down the shades and made sure the door was locked. For safety, I propped it up with the back of a chair. As I did not dare sit at the table which was still visible from the opposite room, I decided to write on the floor. I lay on my stomach and started to work. The first ink worked wonderfully. Before I had time to wait for the ink to dry, I heard some footsteps in the corridor and loud voices. I was sure the police were back. In my panic to finish the life-saving document, no matter what, I filled up the gaping spaces and wrote into them the necessary letters. But the paper was still wet, and the inky letters ran together forming a blotch, making the name illegible. It was the worst, unusable, falsified document.

I felt the earth opening under me. The threatening steps had long since gone away, while I just sat on the floor dumbstruck. It was such a horrible realization that all the trust placed in me, the chances for our escape, the most precious life-saving identification, was destroyed by my clumsiness. My husband would try to escape and if he got out and we met, what then? How could we board a train without his identification papers?

Time was running out. I could not sit there forever. With the utmost effort, I pulled myself together, put away the wretched paper, grabbed my suitcase and left the room.

In my desperation over unsuccessfully falsifying the papers, I did not pay much attention to the clerk. I paid my bill and exited without much further ado.

It was early, about five or six o'clock in the evening. I still had two hours until my date with my husband. I tried to busy myself looking at shop windows, but there was nothing to see. I strolled into a park. I was jumpy and fearful, and my mood was foreboding. Slowly, it started to get cooler outside, and the shadows were getting longer. It was seven o'clock. My suitcase was very clumsy, but the white package with my husband's hat bothered me the most.

Eight o'clock. I was already strolling on the appointed street. Footsteps behind me quickened. A man was approaching. He tilted his hat.

"Are you waiting for someone or could I accompany you?" he asked me politely.

"I have a date," I said. "Do not bother."

He left, but from the corner of my eye I saw that he stopped after some distance and was watching me. I strolled into another street, but I was afraid I would miss my husband. I had to force myself back onto the same street. The man was still waiting at the far end of the street.

Nine o'clock. My husband surely would come any minute now. It became very dark. Only my white paper bag with the hat gave me away. How I wanted to melt into the darkness and become invisible! The man left, and I was relieved. Others came instead. They were circling around me, some of them coming close, peering at me. I was so tired, I felt I would collapse. There was nowhere to go, nowhere to sit.

Ten o'clock. The church chimes sounded again. Some shadowy figures were watching me. I felt the suspicion growing around me. Some tried to talk to me, some gave up right away when I sent them away, but I was watched steadily.

I became numb from the tension, anxiety and constant worry so that I hardly felt my pain-racked limbs anymore. I had probably dozed off on my feet, when the sharp chimes pounded the painful, frightening eleven o'clock into my heart. I was so overcome with desperation I reeled from it. I started to get dizzy. What had happened to my husband? What would become of me? Should I leave on the train alone? No! I had to wait another half hour! How could I leave him? Desert him? How I wished to see him! In my longing I wanted to wring a miracle from heaven; I fervently said my *Tehillim*.

Like in a dream, a figure was approaching from the dark

end of the street. It was coming closer and closer, strange yet familiar. My doubt, my fervent wish formed the approaching figure which grew more familiar with every step. It was him! My husband!

While I was waiting for my husband on that dark street hour after hour, my husband's unit was ordered back to headquarters after work under very strict orders that all the Jewish working brigades prepare themselves for very early morning departure for the Ukraine. They were placed under martial law and warned that any escape attempt meant certain death. No more sick leave, no leaving the premises. Every person was to get his knapsack in order and retire very early for the night.

In the meantime, my husband managed to smuggle the civilian suit I had brought him under his coat, and when the light was out, he changed under the blanket. His closest comrades, who happened to sleep next to him, were petrified by his preparation for his impending escape. They whispered words of admonishment and begged him to desist from his suicidal venture, which would bring destruction to his comrades who would be considered accomplices.

Only one of them, the most *frum* one, begged the others not to discourage him. "Maybe Hashem wants him to be saved," he said.

The painfully slow dressing under the blanket, in drenching perspiration and with a pounding heartbeat, was finally accomplished. Then the army suit had to be pulled over it in case someone spotted him in the army compound.

In the middle of the second layer of dressing, the door swung open without a warning, and the light switch was turned on, flooding the men with its intensity. The officers marched in and began a detailed scrutiny, bunker to bunker, examining the half-asleep working brigade and making head counts. Some of them jumped up from fright, some feigned a deep slumber, among them my husband, whose sleeping form was dangerously bulky. After an unendurable tension-laden time, they stalked out, closing the light and door.

My husband's comrades were sure this unexpected encounter with danger would frighten him, weaken his resolve and finally bring him to his senses. However, this was not the case. He resolutely continued his preparations. He waited and waited until all was still around him, until the tired working brigade was soundly asleep, and hopefully, the guards, too. Then he silently got up and headed in the direction of the latrine. As he walked through the corridors, he unexpectedly bumped into a garbage can, which he sent flying with a crushing sound. He froze, waiting for the inevitable, but nothing happened. As he approached the building which housed the latrine, he saw the gate half open.

The sergeant on watch was leaning on the gatepost playing with a dog. My husband lingered, watching through the holes in the wooden plank of the outhouse. The scene did not change. With a frozen heart, counting the precious hours passing, he waited. The situation seemed hopeless until suddenly, the dog became very playful and ran away from the soldier towards the kitchen. The soldier ran after him. My husband dashed out of the gate to freedom. At the next corner, he took off his uniform.

Hastening his steps and with a trembling heart and body, he was filled with doubts about whether I was still waiting for him in this never-ending dangerous night. On the unknown deserted streets, he made some wrong detours trying to avoid suspicious figures, when he finally found the agreed-upon street and spotted a white bag on a dark, motionless figure which was me.

Gratitude to Hashem overwhelmed us, and we were both sobbing. Then, with renewed strength, we marched towards the railway station. There was no time to waste, since the express was due to leave for Budapest in twenty minutes. My husband looked very dashing, very Aryan, in his hunter hat. A few blocks from the station house, we met an army lieutenant. As he passed us, he heard us giggling (which we thought to be the proper behavior). Then he stopped and our hearts stopped, too, but our feet strolled further. Our keen ears finally picked up the blessed clicking of his army boots as he continued.

Finally, regaining our breath, I blurted out the tragedy of his university certificate's destruction. I explained how through my clumsiness, I messed up the only identification he had. To my relief, he did not take it so tragically. He said that since he had found me nothing could go wrong anymore.

We boarded the train which arrived at the precise moment we entered. Seeing many German soldiers, we decided to join them. We thought them less dangerous than the Hungarians. They would not ask us for identification. We spent a quiet hour in their compartment while the train sped on to Budapest, my husband conversing with them in Hoch Deutsch, which delighted them. Then the conductor entered and angrily ordered us into another section, sternly reproaching us for using the compartment reserved for the German army.

As the first pink glow appeared on the horizon, heralding the unbelievable new day, we were standing by the window and looking at the slowly emerging new sun. With deepest gratitude to Hashem, we uttered the most solemn vow to dedicate our future life and the lives of our future children's to Hashem and His Torah.

We decided to get off at a small station before the main Budapest station, where we hoped for less rigid identification controls. We got off, my husband preceding me, while he purposefully dropped my valise and tried to retrieve it. I hastily put my identification under the policeman's nose, while he blinked into it. The pressure of the crowd behind me pushed us further out . . . into life!

Air Raid over Budapest

■ ■ ■

Moshe Holczler

ONE CANNOT POSSIBLY IMAGINE THE HORROR OF AN AERIAL
bombing if one does not personally live through it. We first experienced it before the Nazi occupation when we were all
together with our family. It came around two o'clock in the
morning. The whole apartment house was awakened from its
deepest slumber as the sirens mercilessly cut into the silent
night. We didn't believe its seriousness and were reluctantly
proceeding half asleep towards the cellar shelters at the end
of the courtyard, angry for the late night drill. We hadn't yet
reached the shelters when a tremendous detonation shook
the ground under us, and the blood froze in our bodies. So this
was it! It's no longer a drill. The next one could strike us.

In no time, everyone was in the shelter, and by the time the
next bomb hit, far away from us, we were following all
regulations like obedient schoolchildren. From that moment
on, we took it very seriously.

This was in early 1943. It was the first Russian bombing

raid on the outskirts of Budapest. As the anti-aircraft batteries started to roar skyward, a blinding aerial torch which hung from a parachute was dropped from one of the planes. The incandescent glow of this so called "Stalin candle" lit up Budapest as if it were noontime. It was finally shot down by a furious concentration of wild bullets, but nonetheless the fear was permanently planted in every Hungarian soul.

Strangely enough, these raids were not repeated at that time, and no aerial raid came during the entire drama of Hungarian deportations in the May-June period of 1944. No matter how much the International Rescue Organization begged the Allied Command from Switzerland to initiate a few air raids against the deportation tracks leading to Auschwitz, not even one air raid came. Nobody but nobody from the outside world disturbed the cruel deportation of the entire Hungarian countryside. Obviously, it wasn't militarily important for thousands of Jewish families to be saved from execution, not for the Russians, nor for the Anglo-American allies.

In the manner of a tragi-comedy, after the entire deportation (excluding Budapest) was completed towards the end of June 1944, a heavy and systematic bombardment of Budapest and its vicinity began. This was interpreted by the Hungarian leadership in one of two ways. Some were convinced it was revenge of Western Jewry for the deportations, and some thought it was a warning against the deportation of the only remaining Budapest Jews. In any event, it made them think twice about what to do with the remaining thousands of Budapest Jews.

They dispensed with the idea of erecting a ghetto, because they imagined that everything would be hit except for the ghetto. Then they wanted to place the concentrated Jew houses in the immediate vicinity of militarily important points to make a Jew umbrella for these targets. Finally, however, when they learned from the first air raids that countless Jews were killed and injured by the Allied bombs, they were convinced that the least important consideration for the Allied bombers was the protection of Jews. They then decided to spread the Jewish houses all over the city, so that the Budapest Jews and gentiles would be equally destroyed. It became obvious that nobody cared for us, neither the Hungarians nor the Western powers.

Still, the general consensus on the streets and among the gentile population was that the Jews had brought this plague on their heads. Whenever bombs fell, curses and abusive remarks against Jews gushed toward the skies. Anti-Semitic violence rose dramatically during and after every bombing raid. One can well imagine how the hiding Jews felt when they were living among these gentiles. It made their situation more vulnerable and dangerous. Jews remaining silent and neutral could make the gentiles more suspicious. An enraged, panic-stricken crowd could lynch them on the spot. The poor Jews didn't know what to fear more, the tremendous danger of the annihilating bombs or the furious hatred of the gentile population.

The simple military explanation for the new bombing sweeps was the fact that the Allied command had invaded and occupied the south and central parts of Italy in 1943. By June, 1944, they were able to organize enough airfields, bombers and supplies in Italy to mount massive raids on Hungarian targets, reaching Budapest from the Yugoslavian border within eight to ten minutes. When Budapest radio reported that enemy planes had crossed the southern border and the city of Baja, everyone started to run for the shelters, not even waiting for Budapest to be alerted.

Within minutes, the picture of the entire capital changed. Private cars headed frantically for the Danube River, crossing bridges toward the hilly section of Duna, where bombings were rare. The Allies didn't bother to fly at night anymore when they discovered that the daytime glare gave them more protection against being seen. They decided that they could hit their targets more accurately by daylight. They came now by the hundreds, in orderly formations, very high, far beyond the reach of anti-aircraft guns. We saw them like hundreds of shiny mosquitoes approaching our airspace with a dreadful and tremendous roar. The entire air trembled from the noise they made. Survival was simply a question of chance or mere luck.

The buses and tramcars stopped in the middle of the streets, just when the first sirens reached them, and everyone cleared out of them in a matter of seconds. There was a public ordinance that every shelter in the city had to admit anybody seeking refuge, and so one never knew in which shelter one would wind up in the next five minutes.

When we arrived in Budapest in the middle of June, 1944, and went into hiding after my wife helped me escape my forced labor unit in Szeged, we fell head-on into the new bombing spree of the Allied air forces. As newcomers, we hadn't yet established our own hiding place, and the family decided we would have to stay temporarily at the apartment of Freily, a Polish refugee with perfect gentile documentation who had been ensconced by the family in a luxurious apartment on Koztelek Street on the Ninth District of Budapest. Freily's job was to hide the two baby boys of the family, disguised as twin girls, her cover story being that they were refugees from another city which was being bombed and that she, as a nurse, was taking care of them.

We were practically forced on her, having no other alternative. She was, however, very indignant about it, because we disturbed her seemingly safe set-up, and we were not reported as residents of the house. I, as an army deserter, had to sleep in a bedding-compartment attached to the ceiling, since I posed a great threat to their safety.

Koztelek Street was the only quiet block between two very busy avenues. Located next to the huge apartment complex was the headquarters of the Gestapo. It was guarded by soldiers with submachine guns. It was quite bizarre, that I, a Jewish army deserter, should hide in a ceiling compartment next door. Indeed, it was so audacious that my wife felt that it might work.

When the daily air-raids began, Freily became a nervous wreck. What should she do if during the air-raid the babies started to cry because they needed to be diapered? If anyone offered to assist her and discovered they were boys, she would be finished! Therefore, she always diapered them at the last minute before descending into the shelter, and all the while, the elevator man would pound on the door for her. Now she had us on her head as an additional menace. What would she say in case of an air-raid?

Once, a raid hit us in mid-afternoon. We told her we were coming down, and she should introduce us to the shelter-commander as one-time visitors who were just caught by the air-raid. She reluctantly consented. The raid didn't last long, but it was enough to discover that the shelter of that house had a terribly dangerous commander. Freily later told us he was a murderer, who had "taken care" of many Jews in the past and was the best friend of one of the high-ranking Gestapo officers.

The commander's face and appearance fit this description perfectly. He had a devilish face and mean, piercing eyes. As the bombs started to fall, he immediately started to shout the most abusive remarks about "those Jews" up there who sent these bombs on them. He repeatedly scrutinized my wife and me, and although we didn't show any sign of it, we felt his scorching gaze on our backs. Luckily, the raid was soon over, but as we arrived upstairs again with Freily and her basket with the twins, we told her we now understood her fears and promised we would never again go down to the shelter with her.

Our resolution not to go down any more was easier said than done. It didn't take a week when, on a sunny day, the radio suddenly alerted the south of Hungary and metropolitan Budapest that a big raid was in the making. Freily hurriedly diapered the babies, watching in pale anticipation to see if we were also preparing for the shelter. We just shook our heads and decided to stick to our resolve. We helped her to the door with the basket, and she left quite relieved, wishing us a safe stay. We heard the quiet humming of the elevator which took her down. We locked the door and sat down in the corner, filled with tension. The sirens still howled while the air trembled and vibrated strongly.

They must be coming in large numbers, we thought, as the awful rumble increased by the minute.

I ran to the street windows and opened each one slightly. We were already familiar with the menace of flying glass chips. The pressure of detonation does much less damage if air penetrates freely. While doing this, I saw that no live soul was on the streets. No vehicles moved. Even the submachine-gun guards of the adjacent Gestapo building had disappeared from sight.

My wife anxiously called me back.

"Get away from there," she warned. "You are giving us away!"

"Who would be crazy enough to watch us now?" I retorted, but I quickly retreated.

Minutes later, the awesome roar increased to a thunder, and a series of bombs began falling. The earth was trembling as the so-called "bombing carpet" headed in our direction with deadly accuracy.

We became pale and frightened. "This time we have really fallen into hell," I said.

We retreated into the bathroom, the only place without windows. Just as we closed the door, a deafening blow hit, and the entire house shook. We believed that the next block was heavily destroyed, and so we tumbled down to the rim of the bathtub to get a hold of something. (We later learned that the entire Bakach plaza, with about fifty buildings, was leveled in that raid.) We felt death close to us as it was obvious we were next to be hit. We closed our eyes, opened our mouths not to get deaf from the air pressure and crouched slightly to save our spines. We already had a thousand regrets that we hadn't gone down to the shelter. A second later, the closest hit thundered alongside. The entire house swayed, and a cracking sound rumbled from the rear. The bathtub tore loose from its mooring.

We completely lost our heads and ran from the apartment, heading for the shelter and hoping we could still reach it; we were just responding to our instinct for survival. As we entered the hallway, another bomb hit, and we saw the entire glass wall of the stairwell split the full length of its five floors. Thousands of glass splinters flew around us, covering all the stairs. We had only gone down half a floor when we realized the glass heaps were impassable. With utter panic, we sat down on our doormat and waited for the end.

But the end didn't come. The roaring sound of planes from above started to subside, and no more bombs fell. We were obviously the last hit as they turned around. As the roar of the enemy planes edged away, we realized that once more, G-d had spared our lives, and we had escaped the fatal pinch.

As we slowly regained consciousness, our instinct prodded us to save ourselves from being caught. We instantly ran the half-flight up to our apartment in order to disappear before civilian calm reasserted itself.

A new scare awaited us. Due to the bombings, the entrance door locked itself tightly when we ran out. My wife recalled hearing a "click" at that moment, and we didn't have a key. Our desperate efforts to open it failed. While the sirens started to blow that all is clear, a new wave of agony befell us. What should we do now?

We knew the house-commander was always the first person to open the iron door of the shelter, and it was his responsibility to check if it was safe to enter the premises. Now that our building itself was hit, he certainly wouldn't clear his charges until he went through the whole house. If he would find us here he would give us away to his friends next door in the Gestapo building. We started to rush down. In desperation, we crashed and slid through the dangerous heap of broken glass. Before we reached the floor below, the iron door-handle grated open.

"Who is upstairs?" a menacing yell was heard. "Is anybody up there?"

We froze stiff, sat down again on the mat and didn't dare move anymore. It seemed we were rescued from the bombs only to fall into the merciless hands of this commander.

There was no way out now.

"No one leaves this shelter until we clear the house with the super," we heard his commanding voice say.

Saying that, they started to climb the stairs by foot, making their assessment of the terrible damages floor by floor. We sat between the fourth and top floors, paralyzed with fear, awaiting our fate. They approached the second floor, the third floor, then somewhat tired, the fourth floor. Our breath almost stopped as we pulled ourselves into the shadow of a door, but we knew this was the end.

As he started to climb the half-floor from the fourth and up, we just closed our eyes. This was the end.

At that moment, we heard his bellowing from just around the bend. "Let's stop here, Andris. It's no use climbing up further. It looks safe enough to let the people up."

Andris agreed and promised to clear away the glass debris as soon as possible. They started to turn around and descend.

"Let's check the motor shaft to see if the elevator is working," we heard them remark. "Everyone should wait for the elevators, because the steps are full of debris."

The Angel of Death, this devilish person, was departing from us. We were completely dazed. For long minutes, we couldn't move or whisper a word.

It took another ten minutes until they checked the power house. We stood up to avoid being seen from the elevators. The first elevator started to rise. We flattened ourselves against the wall and let the first one pass like a silent shadow. It went to the top floor. Soon, we heard Freily emerge. The super was helping her carry the basket with the babies. The babies were crying, and the elevator man speedily closed the door to descend.

Her key was turning in the lock, and as the shadow of the elevator sank alongside us, we ran after her into the cover of the apartment.

The Margit Bridge

■　■　■

Moshe Holczler

IT WAS THE HEIGHT OF NAZI PERSECUTION IN BUDAPEST, WELL
after the Szalasi Revolution of October 15, 1944. Terror filled
the skies over Budapest. The only remaining Hungarian Jews
were jammed into the ghetto of the Seventh District, the only
remaining ghetto in all of Europe. The only other Jews were
concentrated in the so-called "Swedish" or "Swiss" houses or
living in hiding among the Christian population.

My wife and I were also among those who lived under
cover. Our basic driving force was not to accept the fact that
we were denied the right to live, and in this we had tremendous confidence in the help of the Almighty. We had an
apartment in the Obuda section in a newly built apartment
house, registered as a young couple working in the printing
plant of the Capucine Order. Every morning we left the house,
even if we didn't go to work, and just zigzagged the city to
keep up the pretense of being a diligent couple. After the
revolution, however, this going-around became so dangerous

that we did not leave the house, except for going to our job.

One day, frightening news reached us about the planned fate of the ghetto. The Arrow-Cross mob was preparing to surround and ignite the entire ghetto. Our hearts sank. My wife's entire family lived in those houses. It became vital to let them know what was facing them, no matter what kind of danger it posed for us. For someone in hiding to approach the Jewish quarters was doubly dangerous, but there was no way out.

We set out around eleven o'clock in the hopes of arriving there by noon. Our streetcar crossed the Danube River over the prestigious Margit Bridge, and then with a gentle right turn headed towards Pest on the Lopot Boulevard. Our apprehension grew by the minute as we entered the inner city. We chose the nearest stop to the ghetto and got off at the very busy intersection of Rakoczky Avenue. From the rolling crowd we turned unnoticed onto Kazinczy Street, which let into the heart of the ghetto.

We parted. My wife walked ahead, and I followed from a distance. Because the block was quiet at this time of day, we managed to enter unobserved the house where our family lived. As I climbed the stairs in my green hunter hat with my hands in my pocket, whistling, a Jewish woman hastily locked her door from fright. This relieved me and convinced me that my appearance was sufficiently gentile. Finally, we entered the apartment of the family and locked the door firmly behind us. We found them pale, worn and worried although they exhibited joy in seeing us. Then we told them about the immediate dangers facing them.

As they heard the news and our advice that they set up some temporary escape for themselves, they became perplexed and very disturbed. Their only security had come from the knowledge that they were among Jews with whom they shared a common fate, but now their panic grew as they imagined themselves burned alive or shot while escaping.

Finally, they made a decision and promised us to seek refuge for the night in the remote wash-house of their former maid, a last resort that cost them much money.

Relieved that our mission was accomplished and following the same precautions as when we had come, we left the house separately. We turned left in order not to use the same route and headed towards the nearest trolley stop. By the time we realized that by doing so we had to pass the great Orthodox Synagogue of Budapest, we were on the street already, and our hearts started to beat faster. We crossed to the opposite side of the street to avoid the tails of the German Gestapo horses lined up at the entrance, their rears protruding into the street in a deliberate desecration of everything holy for the Jews. Indeed, they used all the synagogues of Budapest for army stables. Without moving a muscle of our faces, we continued with accelerated steps, and only a block later did we allow ourselves a deep sigh at seeing the place of our holiest prayers defaced.

"If only something would happen to give them some troubles to divert their attention from our people," my wife remarked. "They are so relaxed and self-confident. Nothing bothers them. Even the air-raids have subsided in the past few weeks."

As the trolley approached, we both agreed that only some dramatic outburst could save the ghetto from destruction.

In the tramcar we didn't say a word. We just looked out the windows as it speedily cut through the crowded boulevards and turned left to Buda. Leaving the elegant riverfront behind, the tramcar mounted the prestigious Margit Bridge again. The bridge was very crowded. Many trolley lines used it, as well as buses, trucks and pedestrians heading towards the amusements and parks of the ancient Margit Island. While stopping in the middle and discharging a crowd, a disturbing sight caught our eyes.

A galvanized streak of iron cables mounted on supporting

structures, carried brick-shaped metal boxes at regular intervals. Everyone knew they were dynamite charges mounted on all bridge-crossings so that the bridge could be destroyed quickly in case of a sudden enemy advance. Everyone viewed them with trepidation, but every danger becomes commonplace if one is faced with it every day. As the trolley picked up speed, the dynamite rows melted into a long streak and soon disappeared as we reached the other side and turned sharply right toward Buda.

When we reached our stop, it was around two-thirty in the afternoon, a sunny and quiet fall day. We stepped off the streetcar with relief, crossed the tracks and headed towards the steep mountainside toward our apartment house. From afar, about a distance of five to six miles, we heard the steady rumbling noise of the Margit Bridge with the faint tinkling of the tramcar bells and puffing of the autobus mufflers.

We climbed and stopped to rest for a few minutes when suddenly something terrible happened. Like an earthquake, the rocks shook beneath us, and a tremendous detonation rumbled through the air as if several aerial bombs exploded at once.

Our feet remained rooted to the ground. We hastily turned to the far right from where the astonishing sound came. There was a huge black cloud rising above the Danube River from the direction of the Margit Bridge. Windows were thrown open and people stared out of them. Others ran out of doorways, bewildered. What had happened? There was no air-raid and no alarm from the radio.

At this instant, police sirens and ambulances could be heard speeding in the direction of the Margit Bridge. Huge army trucks pulled out of a nearby army barrack, loaded with combat-ready troops, carrying machine guns and hand grenades.

Seeing this unusual disturbance we felt we had better disappear from the crowd and go up to our apartment.

Coming upstairs with palpitating hearts, we opened the radio.

"Attention! Attention!" the announcer shouted. "A terrible criminal act has occurred. The Margit Bridge was detonated by subversive elements. All police emergency units are to contact their headquarters for instructions. Take positions at all bridge approaches and control batteries. Everyone remain calm and do not approach the bridge. All emergency wards at the hospital prepare to treat the injured. Army and navy rescue squads proceed to the Margit Bridge. Wait for further instructions!"

We sat there in silence, astonished and trembling.

"My G-d!" I exclaimed. "We just came off that bridge twenty minutes ago. Can this be true? All those people?"

It was just too much to digest and believe. As the hours passed, it became apparent that it was true. We didn't know what to be thankful for first, our own escape or the dramatic blow to Budapest which would probably divert attention from the Jews of the ghetto.

"Your wishes became a prophecy!" I said as I turned to my wife with excitement. "You complained that nothing troubles them, that they have too much time to plan against the Jews. Now they got it! Now they have what to be busy with!"

"Thank G-d a thousand times," she whispered. "But be very careful now that you don't show happiness or satisfaction. We can't even tell anyone we just came off that bridge. They might even suspect we had something to do with it. At such a time, everyone is a suspect."

The dramatic hours that followed, well into the night and the next morning, revealed that the Margit Bridge had indeed been exploded by its prepared dynamite charges when someone had shorted the electric circuit. In the midst of the heaviest traffic, the bridge broke into several segments, discharging all its traffic into the watery grave of the Danube River. Trolley cars jammed with people went right into the water. Buses, trucks and pedestrians all fell to their deaths to the water below. Such a brutal blow had never occurred in Budapest before. Thousands of people died, and corpses were being pulled from the icy waters for many days following the explosion. The tramway cars, buses and trucks were not pulled out until many months and years had passed, well after the liberation of Budapest.

From then on, all bridges were very heavily guarded day and night. The investigations revealed that the Communist underground was responsible for the blast, and an exhaustive manhunt began, starting with the known Communist hideouts. *Baruch Hashem*, they didn't accuse the Jews, because that would have been the worst tragedy for them.

This unbelievably providential act averted the immediate danger for the Jews in the ghetto. Budapest was thrown into confusion for months following this trauma. This was the first cold-blooded reminder that the Russian front was nearing, and the self-confidence of the Germans evaporated.

My wife and I felt like Lot and his family when they fled from Sodom. We were afraid to look back! As for myself, ever since our experience, I can never cross a bridge without anxiety and saying "thank you" when I am safely on the other side.

Do You Have Seven Pennies?

■ ■ ■

Sarah Holczler

ON A SPARKLING SUNNY AFTERNOON IN NOVEMBER, 1944, IN OLD
Buda, my cousin Rachel, my husband and I discussed the
possibility of taking the trip to Pest to visit my sister's children,
who were being hidden by a gentile for a fortune of money.
My only sister had been arrested by the Gestapo and her
husband deported, leaving us the loving substitute-parents for
the children.

By then, Szalasy, the Hitler-like leader of Hungary, was in
full power, and according to his decree, any Jew found hiding
would be executed on the spot. Despite this, our hearts urged
us on, fearing for the fate of these children, and we embarked
on the trip. We agreed upon a secret phrase to alert one
another in case of recognition by a passersby or fellow
passenger. The phrase was, "Do you have seven pennies?"

We were in disguise, effecting gentile outfits, posture and
behavior, which we had studied thoroughly. We boarded the
first tramcar. The train barely made a few stops when a group

of college students embarked, wearing their familiar caps. With a sinking heart, I recognized one of them from my little town. He belonged to a family which was virulently anti-Semitic even in peacetime, but we had played together as children. I asked for "seven pennies" from my husband, and we got off at the next station without haste.

I wondered if he had indeed recognized me and, even if he had, if he would have harmed me seeing that I was obviously pregnant.

We continued walking in the same direction towards the next stop, deeply engrossed in our heartache over my sister's fate. Suddenly, we caught sight of the same group heading towards us on the narrow sidewalk. They had evidently gotten off at the next stop and were ominously and purposefully approaching us like Angels of Death.

"Rachel," I whispered to my cousin. "Please step away from us and go into the next street. They want us! Tell the family what happened."

My cousin quickly walked away, just before the three boys and one girl came face to face with us.

"Aha!" my former playmate said. "I know you!"

They came behind our backs and trailed us closely. We did not utter one word.

It was a narrow and sparsely populated area of the Busa Main Street, but further up stood the Likacs Sap, a large building occupying many square blocks. on that corner, a fearful gendarme stood with fixed bayonet and shotgun. Now we understood their plan. They wanted us to reach that point before they would act.

"Let's hurry to the left and get away from Main Street and down to the Danube shore," my husband whispered urgently as we approached the corner.

We crossed the street and ran into a side street.

"Jews! Catch them!" our pursuers started to yell.

In the fleeting, terrifying moment, I saw the gendarme

grab his shotgun, but by that time we were running unabash-
edly next to the unending walls of the Lukacs Sap towards the
Danube.

The cobblestone street echoed with our running feet
which was deafened only by my heartbeat. How could I
outrun my enemy while I was pregnant? My knees started to
buckle and sharp piercing pains cut into my womb. My
husband was urging me on, trying to give me strength to go
faster. I did not hear anything; only my blurred eyes saw walls
swimming before me. I slowly began to black out, when out
of nowhere, a brown spot appeared on the cruel, unending
walls. It was a wooden door. With the last breath of a dying
victim, I thrust hard and it opened.

We fell into the courtyard of the bathhouse where people
lounged on beach chairs. At first, we rushed through the
intricate corridors, but then we came to our senses and
slowed down so as not to attract more attention. There was no
more strength left in us, but we knew we couldn't remain
concealed. The miraculous respite was just temporary, as we
knew our tormentors would not stop. In order to catch a Jew,
the whole bath-house could be cordoned off. We had witnessed such horrors elsewhere. Just to kill one more Jew!

We had to leave our temporary sanctuary. There was only
one way out, back to the same Main Street. Holding our
breaths, we arrived at the gate and crossed the same street and
hurried across to the first courtyard, just to escape our
hunters' eyes. Our steps echoed once again on cobblestones
into the courtyard, and a uniformed pilot officer pounced
upon us.

"What do you want?" he demanded.

"Oh, please, officer," I said. "I desperately need a bathroom!"

"There is nothing here," the officer replied. "It is a re-
stricted place. Get out immediately!"

We turned towards the street again, knowing full well that

by this time our pursuers would arrive at the opposite side. Suddenly, a tramcar, sent from heaven, rushed towards us. By the time we approached, it started to close it's doors. I grabbed the closing door. My nails desperately clutched the automatic doors and slid off. The tramcar left us. We were standing there annihilated, deathbound, when like in a dream, the vanishing tramcar stopped and started to back up towards us.

The driver must have seen our despair. The doors opened and we forced our stiff, immobile legs to enter its blissful embrace. The tramcar silently sped away with us.

Later, we found out from Rachel, who had followed us from a distance, that as we boarded the heaven-sent tramcar to our final escape, the three would-be murderers ran out of the Lukacs Spa with a group of Jew-hunters, frantically searching for us.

Light Signals

■ ■ ■

Sarah Holczler

IT WAS ONE OF THOSE EVENINGS WHEN WE HAD TO PREPARE THE
scene in our living room for the casual, carefree life of gentiles.
The table was spread with playing cards, some half-empty
liquor bottles, glasses, and an ashtray with cigar ashes.

The French window in our modern apartment was heavily
curtained in accordance with the blackout order of the police.
Very heavy fines were levied for the slightest ray of light
escaping to the outside.

Cousin Rachel, whom we called Cousin Anne, and Cousin
Yechezkel, whom we called Uncle Feri, were staying with us
in our apartment in a brand new building in Buda, the only
available apartment at that time. The apartment contained an
unfinished closet space in the kitchen over which we had
placed a specially fitted cabinet, leaving a hiding place behind
it. My husband was not only a Jew-in-hiding but also a fugitive
from the army. After his miraculous escape from the army, his
name and photograph were displayed in many police and

army stations with a huge reward offered for his capture. We decided that in the event of a raid on our apartment he would hide in that empty pre-arranged space.

Uncle Feri had excellent false papers as a teacher, as did Anne and, to a lesser degree, my husband and I. We also had a prearranged well-ringing formula for family members who might want to come to us in cases of extreme emergency.

We were well aware that we could not run to the air raid shelters in case of an air-raid. We just could not risk the scrutiny of the tenants, and mostly the feared Nazi informer-superintendent (those were the commandants of every building) who would have ample time to scrutinize our features and question us as new tenants. Therefore, the evenings were even more tense that the days, if that is possible to imagine, because of the double danger. Still, we preferred to die by a bomb rather than by the hands of cruel humans.

As this particular evening progressed, with a brief air raid emergency around ten p.m., the bell suddenly rang! We froze. There was some scraping of shoes and some whispering. I went to the door and opened the latch. There stood the broken, trembling figure of Bela, my sister's brother-in-law.

I quickly opened the door and welcomed the unshaven, blackened and filthy young man inside. He was almost incoherent as he told us he had been hiding in a coal cellar for two weeks. He had run out of food and water, and since his discovery seemed imminent, he decided he could not stay there anymore. He was completely famished and weakened.

We were desperate. We knew that he would be our undoing, because he really looked like the "fugitive Jew," with no identification papers. But was his life less valuable than ours? We let him have a quick bath, food and shelter.

We retired for the night with the fervent hope that Hashem would watch over us doubly, in the *zchus* of the big *mitzvah* of taking care of this dangerous, unwanted guest.

Suddenly, the bell started ringing with a shrill, prolonged

intensity. Knees buckling, I dragged myself to the door and opened the latch. Before I could peer out, the barrel of a machine gun was shoved against my chest (in my mind I can still see the many-holed round metal of the machine gun). A rough voice ordered me to open the door immediately.

Not heeding the order, I quickly switched off the hall light and rushed back into the living room. While they tried to force our door, I hastily pulled my husband through the dark hall into the empty hiding place in the kitchen. With Uncle Feri's help, I closed the opening and secured my husband behind it. Then I hurried back to the door to receive the *Malach Hamaves*. Fumbling with the lock, I opened the door with trembling hands.

Two state troopers roughly knocked me over with the door.

"Why did it take so long to open the blasted door?" they barked into my face.

"You frightened me out of my wits with your machine gun," I stammered. "Are you surprised I lost my head? This is no way to enter a peaceful citizen's apartment at night!"

They did not listen and rushed into the living room, straight to the window, pulled the curtain apart and snooped around. Then they faced Uncle Feri and Anne, who were holding the playing cards frozen in their hands. Feri pulled himself together with amazing dignity. Reacting coolly to the order to show his identification papers, he took out his wallet and showed his papers with impressive calmness. His school-teacher papers were in order, and so were Anne's.

"What is the raid for?" Uncle Feri asked with cold politeness.

"We were informed," one of them growled, "that spies are hiding in this apartment. They saw light signals blazing from these windows, directing enemy planes."

We froze as they ran to every window, opening doors and closets and peering under beds. Remembering Bela, I nearly fainted! The dangerous guest! Where had he hidden? I felt that if this went on for one minute longer, they would find him and we would be finished.

Suddenly, the kitchen door opened, and my husband's ghost-like figure appeared. White like a sheet, in a daze, he came forward with wooden legs. The impact was tremendous. The state troopers were aghast, and so were we.

"And who is this?" one of them demanded.

My husband whispered something to the effect that he was asleep and had just woken up. He showed them his identification papers.

With aroused suspicion, they scrutinized his papers at length. I felt the atmosphere reach a breaking point and knew that they would not be satisfied with a fruitless search after breaking into a gentile apartment. They had to produce something or else they would lose face.

All through this agonizing procedure, I was lacing my high shoes which I had taken off for the night, ready to drag myself out during the late term of my pregnancy to the execution squad. This unbelievable detail preoccupied my mind as I mentally prepared for death.

Suddenly, a thought came to me out of desperation.

"Oh, I know what the officer and the people may have seen from the window," I cried out. "You must be right! Just beneath our apartment, is an apartment with the exact same layout as ours, and it is empty. Please let me show it to you. Come with me."

Hearing these words, they looked at each other and I felt the tension subside in them. One of them leaned towards me.

"Let's try," he said.

With these words and an immense sense of relief that I was leaving my loved ones blissfully protected, we marched out of the apartment with me leading the two murderous troopers downstairs. I showed them the empty apartment. The unfinished floor was strewn with straw and our eyes could make out the shape of footsteps leading to the uncovered span of a French window. I pointed out the sure signs to them and one of them seconded my findings.

"You see Jani, these are the real signs of a spy working here," he remarked. "It is a good nest for that rascal. We will surround the whole building and not a soul will leave before we find the spy!"

"I truly hope," I said, "that you will find the devil who dares to give us away to the enemy. I wish you good hunting and a good night, officers."

With those words, I parted from them. Going back up into our apartment was like entering life itself. To see the relief in their eyes showed that they had not known whether or not they would see me alive again.

We found Bela in the bathroom, drenched in his own cold perspiration, sitting in the tub covered by the curtain. How many times had the officers opened the very same door? It was truly a miracle of Hashem!

My husband then explained his reason for leaving the hiding place. When he heard the intensive, hostile search, he became panicky, afraid that they would find him, which would mean a sure death for him and the rest of us as well. The confining little place became hotter and hotter, until the growing fear became unbearable, and he decided to sneak out and show himself.

We spent the night in a vigil, knowing that the troopers' threat was not an empty one. There was no way of knowing if we would be able to leave the house in the morning.

The morning came. We prudently waited until midmorning until all the officers left the house. There was no trace of the night troopers, and we all escaped, never to return to that apartment again.

Five Minutes of Chanukah

■　■　■

Moshe Holczler

NOBODY WAS SURE IF THERE WOULD BE A *CHANUKAH* FOR THEM that winter. it was the beginning of December, 1944, in tumultuous Budapest, beleaguered by German tanks, Gestapo agents and Arrow-Cross hordes under the shadow of an advancing Russian army. The clouds of death floated over the city, which instead of concentrating on its defense, turned against the last remaining Jews from all of Europe. The craze of hatred filled the streets, and finally, even the gentile population was horrified by the atrocities of the Szalasi mob.

My wife and I were hiding under the most fantastic circumstances. We were employed as a gentile couple at the printing plant the Capucine Convent. Somehow, we felt more secure hiding among priests. I was employed as a typesetter, and my wife was in the stock room working on the paper sheets.

All the Nazi leaflets were printed in our printing shop on the Buda Main Street, while we were secretly living on the fourth floor of a nearby apartment house. We became the caretakers of a luxurious apartment that belonged to a lieutenant-colonel of the Hungarian army. He fled to the West and sublet his entire apartment to us in the hope that we would save it from the Russians. My wife was pregnant, and they hoped that the Russians would not bother a working couple with a baby on the way. Our only worry was that they left behind their faithful maid who acted as a spy under the pretext of keeping the apartment in good shape. She jeopardized our privacy completely, but the richness of the home and its relative security offset this nuisance. Our camouflage seemed to be so perfect that all valuables of our own dispersed family were brought into this apartment.

Our bearded Capucine monk bosses, in their brown cowls, woven girdles and wooden sandals, were the only gentiles who were undisturbedly happy during those times. Their full-mouthed laughs and violent oaths filled our work place. One day in early December, the chief Prelate appointed my wife to go shopping with him the following week for a nice Yuletide tree.

That year, *Chanukah* was supposed to start on December 11. On Sunday, the day before *Chanukah*, we were home in our "gentile fortress," and as the hours neared to sundown, we got an irresistible urge to partake, even if only slightly, in the spirit of *Chanukah*. We were terrified by the terrible risk, but nevertheless, we started to plan carefully. My wife's cousin was our guest and brought along two candles. We found the only supermarket open on Sunday and sent the maid shopping.

As the sun set, we draped the windows of the small utility room and locked the doors. In the pitch darkness, I lit the *shames* to say the three *berachos* of the first light. At *Shehecheyanu*, our eyes filled with tears! We then sang *Maoz Tzur*, and after five minutes of sheer heaven, we extinguished the two lights, carefully cleaned up all traces and aired out the room.

By the time the maid returned from shopping, we were sitting in the dining room as if nothing had happened. Only our heart palpitations could have given us away.

The next day, my wife was scheduled to go tree-shopping with the Capucine Prelate. Some assignment for the first day of *Chanukah*! But fate decided differently.

On that sunny morning, we had just returned from the coffee break, and I was busy with the lead lines, when suddenly our foreman came out of the machine room.

"Gentlemen, everyone is asked to come to the office with their documents," he announced with a big, sad face. "We have a military control raid."

Naturally, all work stopped. We saw the military policemen, accompanied by the well-known cruel Hungarian gendarmes and some regular city policemen, seal all entrances. I didn't want to show any alarm but felt the blood rushing to my head. I went to the locker for my papers, but some instinct told me not to pick up my jacket, because I might need it as an excuse later.

I was very worried about the reliability of the army discharge papers I had bought for so much money with the help of my wife's family. I knew that an inspection by these officers was a serious matter, even for a gentile. We were in the midst of the Szalasi revolution, well after the deportation of the Hungarian Jews, when every able gentile man was on the battlefronts; anyone in civilian clothes was risking his life if he did not have perfect documents to cover him. A Jew hiding amongst the gentiles, six months after the deportations, was likely to be shot on the spot without any mercy or pity. The risk was terrible, and here I was, facing my first raid.

I crossed the paper-room to my wife.

"Take your things and go home immediately," I tensely whispered, "because I don't know what will come out of this. I don't want to be handicapped if I have to run."

She looked at my deathly pale face and quietly started for

the dressing room. I entered the office and stood in line behind the other men, seemingly indifferent. My colleagues were released one after the other so I was a bit relieved. When it was finally my turn, the officer looked at my paper with searching eyes, because I was too young to be at home.

Then he tossed it back to me with a piercing look.

"It is no good!" he declared. "The date is already invalid!"

I felt the floor open under me as he directed me to step into the corner until he finished with the others. I knew that if I were to wait for an interrogation, I would be finished. I looked around desperately, only to see the grim faces of the gendarmes and the bewildered look of the Capucine monk who was in charge of the printing plants. As a last resort, my gaze turned to the only policeman present who seemed a little more humane than the others present. Somehow, I discovered a bit of compassion in his eyes, as he saw, by my pale face, that I was in a dangerous fix. I gathered up my courage and addressed him.

"Oh! I just remembered!" I said. "I have a re-examining paper of a later date."

"And where is it?" he asked.

"In my jacket in the dressing room," I replied.

"So bring it at once!" was the angelic reply. (Until this very day, I am convinced that Eliyahu Hanavi was disguised as that policeman.)

The officer overheard his words.

"You stay here!" he exclaimed with a commanding tone. "Don't go anywhere!"

I was desperate. I felt the last hope fading away. This evil man was picking on me and holding me in his iron fist. A few minutes later, however, he was called to the telephone by his commander, and using this lull, the friendly policeman quietly signalled me to go and get my paper. I went as unobtrusively as possible, sending him a message of deep gratitude with my eyes. Coming out of that terrible office, I rushed to pick up my jacket and then entered the toilet. I locked the door and peeked through the window to the rear of the building. No one was there.

I jumped through the window and ran up to the side street, into the hallway of our apartment house. I rushed up the four flights and frantically rang the bell. To my luck, my wife came to the door and not the old gentile maid whom the previous owner had forced upon us to watch over his furnishings. If she would have seen my face then, all could have been lost. I almost couldn't talk from panic, as I told my wife to come right away, as is, or everything might be lost!

Frightened, she grabbed her coat, and we ran down to the lobby. There was only one exit, and it posed a great danger for us. It opened into the plaza at the front of the convent. We peered anxiously through the glass door, covered by the shadow, to see if any of the gendarmes were out there. Seemingly, they hadn't yet discovered my escape, but it could happen at any second. This was the most crucial moment, but there was no other alternative. We had to take the risk.

We stepped out and hastily bypassed the plaza and hurried up the winding streets to the mountainside. We didn't care where we were going, we just wanted to get away from there. We crisscrossed streets and blocks, and everything was flying before our eyes in a frenzy. We climbed steadily higher, between hidden villas and quiet estates, helped by the noontime rest of the inhabitants. At a very distant point, we had to stop to catch our breath.

"Do you realize that we lost everything?" my wife told me with anguish. "Our home, our jobs, our clothing. I even left my purse with our food ration card with the address of our other hideout. What will be with us now?"

"Let's make sure we don't lose our lives!" I muttered.

Below us, a beautiful valley unfolded in painful contrast to our misery. Suddenly, my wife pointed to the backyard of a villa under us.

"Look!" she exclaimed. "A woman is hanging out her laundry!"

We watched with broken hearts as the woman carelessly hung her clothing on the line on this sunny, breezy December morning, like the most natural privilege of a housewife.

"She is not afraid of anything," said my wife, unable to suppress her bitterness. "She has a home . . . she is sure and secure . . . and we are running for our lives! Will I ever be able to hang out my wash without fear like this gentile woman does? Will I ever wash laundry at all?"

Only the wind was there to answer, as we continued our escape in a panic. We sped away with the next trolley towards the other end of Budapest, where we had reserved a furnished room for emergencies. Our desperation was boundless. There was an unspoken question in our minds. Was this the reward for our *Chanukah* sacrifice?

Heading towards the furnished room, my wife recalled once again that she had left her handbag with the food cards bearing our new address on them. So not only did we have no food, but we had left strong evidence leading to our whereabouts.

It was cold and damp, late in the afternoon, and we had no place to go. We wandered for many hours, not daring to approach the apartment, because of the give-away address left behind. Finally, having no choice, we entered, beaten and dead tired, and lay down on the couches with rumbling stomachs until our bachelor landlord arrived. We told him that we just arrived from Transylvania and that our belongings would arrive tomorrow. We lay down, tense and worried. Who knew if they would come for us? My pregnant wife was shaking from hunger until exhaustion overcame us and we fell asleep.

Two o'clock at night, we were awakened by a piercing bell and the rumbling sound of a car.

They are here for us, the thought echoed through our

dazed, half-asleep consciousness. In panic, we dragged ourselves to the window to jump. Our landlord answered the
door, and we heard a mailman through the slot.

"I have a telegram for Kalman Nagy," said the mailman.

With great relief, we fell down on our couch. Ten minutes
later, a soft knock was heard at our door. It was the landlord.
He was as pale as the wall.

"I am so sorry to disturb you," he said, "but I just got an
urgent call from my army unit. I must pack up and go at six
o'clock in the morning. It's lucky you came now. I leave my
entire apartment to you. You can use whatever you want.
Take good care of everything, and you'll pay me later."

We felt as if the heavens had opened up for us once again.
This was a genuine miracle. Starving and without food cards,
we were offered a fully furnished home for our own use.

Our landlord took us to his pantry and showed us hanging
salamis, frankfurters and sausages up to the ceiling, all *treif*, of
course. My wife immediately looked for something we could
use. She found a few potatoes, onions and dried beans. We
almost couldn't wait until the morning.

Our landlord was sad to go but still happy that we remained in his house. As soon as he was gone, we burned out
a gas range, making it kosher. For breakfast, we had some
warm potatoes cooked in a thin jar.

One danger was eliminated. We had an apartment filled
with clothing, linen, everything. We saw how blind we were
when we thought Hashem had forsaken us.

A week later, we found out through a telephone call from
a city telephone booth that the entire house in Buda had been
closed by the army and police after we left, and that the
detectives were still waiting for us to return. Two days after
we left, a cannon shell hit the roof of that house and ripped off
the front walls. This was the second miracle for us, but the
menace of the food cards we had left behind still remained.

One week later, on the Yule night, fierce shelling began

and lasted throughout the following day. The Russian army overran Budapest at Szekesfehervar and encircled Budapest. The next day, they advanced to the Danube River, attacking the section of Buda which includes the Capucine Convent and our former home. The site became the scene of house-to-house fighting. All bridges of the Danube River were detonated, and Pest was completely cut off from Buda. Thus, the menace of the abandoned food cards was also gone.

We then realized that what we had thought our greatest tragedy had actually been our greatest miracle. Had we not been chased out of there, we would have perished in those fierce battles. We said a heartfelt thank to Hashem for our escape.

And all this, in the merit of those five minutes of *Chanukah* lights.

My Friend Erzsi

■ ■ ■

Sarah Holczler

AMONG THE WOMEN WHO WERE WORKING AT THE PLANT MY
husband described in the previous chapter was Erzsi, a young
Catholic girl. She was engaged to a soldier, who came quite
often and waited for her to finish the job. Many times I
watched them as they left together, so carefree and gay, and
I wondered how anyone could be so carefree in these dreadful
times.

Erzsi was rather plain looking, with a very bad complex-
ion, but she had a very appealing high spirit. She constantly
joked and laughed. I felt a kind of friendship towards her
because of her warmth, in sharp contrast to the others, and
because she showed some measure of good will towards me.

The printing plant was situated alongside the Danube
River, and from this vantage point, we often witnessed the
horrible sight of Jews herded in endless columns along the
riverside under the watchful eyes of machine-gun-wielding
Nazi storm troopers. On these occasions all work stopped,

and the workers crowded around the glass doors and shrieked with pleasure as they ogled the gruesome sight. I had to show interest as well, while inside my heart was breaking. On one occasion, I was watching Erzsi's face as she was witnessing another death march. She was so cheerful I could have throttled her.

The next morning, policemen came into the plant and asked for large sheets of paper to cover the corpses left alongside the river. No one showed any pity, least of all, the Capucine monks. Their incessant merrymaking, loud laughter and drinking contaminated the atmosphere. That day, I was "honored" to accompany the chief Capucine father to shop for Yuletide trees.

Suddenly, the entrance door was darkened by three Nazi storm troopers. They came into the plant and barked an order to all the male workers to line up for identification. The story of our escape is already told in the previous chapter.

Several days after our narrow escape, we decided to take a risk and contact Erzsi by phone because we needed to know the extent of the search for us and if our home, which held all our worldly possessions, had been discovered. I felt that Erzsi was the only decent person in whom we could trust. As we made the call, we trembled with the fear that somebody might overhear the conversation and trace it to us.

Speaking in a disguised voice, I asked the clerk at the plant for Erzsi. She came to the phone, and her first reaction was to catch her breath and mumble something incoherent. Using my true voice, I asked whether anyone was within earshot. Erzsi assured me that no one was nearby. I beseeched her to meet me near the fountain in the Varosliget Park. Erzsi promised to come alone and in total secrecy.

After a sleepless night, the next day finally dawned. My husband and I arrived at the park at the appointed time, and we mingled with the crowds. My husband then hid behind a statue, where he could scan the whole area for any signs of a trap. I sat down on the fountain base.

Suddenly, I saw her approaching. My heart jumped so wildly I was afraid it would tear my ribs out. She was walking at a leisurely pace, but when she caught sight of me, she ran towards me and hugged me.

"You crazy little woman," she whispered in my ear. "My dear little sister, I am Jewish like you! You did not feel it? I knew you were Jewish the first minute you stepped into our plant."

The whole park started to spin with me. "It is a dream!" I gasped. "It is a dream!"

"You gave yourself away so many times, I had to cover up for you with some joke," she continued.

I was speechless. We cried and laughed and hugged. When finally we wiped our tears and calmed down, my husband appeared from his hiding place.

"My G-d!" I exclaimed. "Finally, I found a good Christian and it turned out to be a Jew!"

After we reassured her that she was really a perfect "shiksa," she told us that her "soldier boyfriend" was her Jewish cousin.

Returning to the purpose of our meeting, she sadly informed us that within five minutes of our escape the printing place became a stirred beehive. The police put a cordon around the building, and when someone reported that our apartment was nearby, the police put a security net around the entire five-story apartment house. Unfortunately, a few Jews hiding in the building were caught in the net and taken away.

A Lump of Sugar

■ ■ ■

Sarah Holczler

AT THE END OF DECEMBER, 1944, WE HID AS CHRISTIANS IN OUR rented apartment. The two giant armies, German and Russian, were locked in a deathly embrace over our heads. Fierce infantry fighting, supported by shells and mortars, shook the walls of our building, and we trembled within our shelter walls. It was a house to house, room to room unceasing struggle to the death.

The established tenants in the apartment house were entrenched in the safest part of the shelter. As newer tenants, we were assigned a place on a makeshift deck, which was almost at street level. Everyone took couches and mattresses down from their apartments to the shelter.

From the very beginning, we were looked upon with suspicion as intruders, in spite of our cover story that we were fugitives from Transylvania escaping the Russians. Besides the unending fear of the bombs and shelling and fear of being discovered as Jews, we were desperately hungry. All around us, people who had anticipated the storming of the capital had hoarded ample foodstuffs, but we hugged a few dry beans to our hearts.

Suddenly and unexpectedly, there was a lull from the bombs exploding, and the chattering machine guns ceased. Above us was a mezzanine which contained a small kitchen with four bare walls, a tiny window near the whitewashed ceiling and a stove with two gas burners. Hugging my small saucepan, I ventured up to the kitchen with my precious handful of dry beans. Another woman, seeing my bravery, followed me with the same idea. She was, however, one of the established tenants. She roughly motioned to me to take the outer ring of the stove, which was directly under the tiny window. I had no right to protest.

So what? I thought. It's only one more degree of danger. It doesn't matter. Just let the beans swell and grow while cooking. Let them swell and grow to fist size each!

"No meat?" the woman asked cruelly.

"Oh, I cannot stand the smell of meat," I explained, "being that I am pregnant."

We watched the tiny flames and bubbling water. Suddenly, there was a tremendous ear-splitting shriek from her. She swayed as blood spurted from her arm and sprayed the white walls. We screamed for help. By the time the men rushed up from the shelter, she was lying on the floor, writhing and screaming in pain. Later, we realized that a bullet had smashed through the tiny window and ricocheted from the wall straight into her arm.

All night long, she moaned, delirious with fever. "Why me?" she repeated endlessly. "Why not the other? Why me? Why not the other?"

Hashem! Endless *chessed*!

The next day dawned. It was ominously quiet; our ears could not fathom it. Someone suggested going to the upper corridor to catch some fresh air, stretch our atrophied muscles

and exercise, as we couldn't stand up in our cubicle. Hardly
had we begun to enjoy our upright positions and the fresh
new air when a tremendous swishing sound shook the building. Unbelievable air pressure threw us against the wall. To
our amazement, we saw an enormous hole cut by a falling
torpedo through the whole length of the corridor from one
end to the other, about two feet from our heads. The torpedo
then fell down with a crushing sound and was quiet. We crept
back into our shelter, not quite believing what our eyes had
seen.

Later, the superintendent reported that a torpedo the size
of a table was resting in our bathroom, and it was likely to
explode any minute. Everyone knelt and prayed. After another day, my husband sneaked upstairs and *davened* undisturbed next to the torpedo. Later, he hid his *tefillin* and *siddur*
there with the bomb, since no one dared go near it.

Several days later, still imprisoned in our shelter but alive,
we heard loud voices speaking in foreign guttural sounds. We
were elated! At last, the Russians had arrived and were in
control, hopefully, of the city!

The voices grew louder. Someone was forcing the trap
door leading to our cellar shelter. My husband felt it would be
appropriate to show friendliness and greet the new lords of
our life. As he climbed the steps, a huge, seven-foot monster
appeared at the trap door. When my husband bowed in
deference, the monster grabbed his neck and threw him to
the ground. Then snarling something unintelligible, he showed
the terrified people his machine guns, producing click-clack
sounds with them. That introduced the new dawn of our era.

Day and night, the Russians forced their way into our
shelter, lining up the men. "*Davay, davay!*" they shouted,
ordering them out to help push trucks and guns into the firing
line of battle that was still raging. My husband was caught, but
he escaped from them on the streets.

Whenever the fear subsided momentarily, the gnawing

hunger tortured us. Only one craving drove me crazy–to have one lump of sugar. I dreamed of it. Nice, sparkling, white squares of sugar lined up in front of my eyes, but when I hungrily reached for them, they rolled away, growing smaller and smaller until they completely disappeared.

One morning, a loud banging on the shelter's trap door woke us up. In marched two Mongol giants. The pair ordered us from our cramped sleeping quarters. Their method of communication was very direct. They grabbed the first person at hand and sent him sprawling, whereby everyone hurried to avoid the same fate.

It seemed they were looking for hidden guns and ammunition, and our flimsy mattresses were no match for their huge boots. Everything went flying until they came to my neighbor, an old grumpy man lying on his elevated sleeping place. We had always wondered about the chest he used as a makeshift bed. He never talked but just lay there like an old dog guarding a bone.

The big boots gave a mighty heave, and the old man, who tenaciously clung to his pad, rolled off. But his solid oak chest was exposed, and an angry kick turned it over. There, to our amazed eyes, were a million lumps of sugar cascading in all directions. White, shiny sugar!

The soldiers became quite human in their laughter. Only the old man snarled. I yearned for one lump of sugar, but of course, he would not give me even one. I could have grabbed, but I did not touch any. The old dog crawled all day to collect his hoard, every last bit of it. Nobody touched it. There was no giving, but there was no taking either.

The next day, in the early afternoon, the Russians came to look for men as helpers for the soldiers. By that time, none of the men previously taken had returned to their families. The soldiers saw my husband, who was the only young man left.

"*Davay, davay, Niemetzky*! Come, German," they barked their command. (My husband had reddish blond hair and looked not only Christian but German.)

Deathly pale, my husband got up from the bench. A little boy, whose mother had been forcibly taken out by the soldiers the previous night, happened to be sitting next to my husband. The child gave a hysterical nerve-shattering shriek which froze the soldiers. Thinking that the boy was my husband's son, they took pity on him and motioned my husband to go back to the little boy. This was one more miraculous *chessed* from Hashem who helped us without end through the depths of our sufferings.

The Night in the Forest

■ ■ ■

Moshe Holczler

A FEW DAYS AFTER OUR LIBERATION FROM THE NAZIS BY THE
Russian troops in the middle of January, 1945, we ventured
out of our shelter on the Bazskay Street of the Budapest Zuglo
district to search for surviving members of the family, especially the two baby boys left in the custody of the "Freily" in
the luxurious apartment house on Koztelek Street.

At that time, we didn't realize how dangerous our venture
was. As we crossed the first plaza, a strafing bullet barrage
barely missed us, as we heard their crackling hits around us on
the pavement. Only then did we see that people all around,
hiding in doorways, were watching in horror as we crossed.

Naturally, we continued cautiously, seeking cover and
running only when no planes were heard overhead. There
was no transportation. All over, people were still in the
shelters. The streets were covered with ruins, road blocks,
burned vehicles and huge piles of frozen garbage. Filth and
decay lay all around. The winter snow and ice was a blessing

now, a protection against an outbreak of disease.

We arrived at the huge building, the target of an air-raid in which we had almost lost our lives. We inquired about the old nurse with the two baby girls.

"Yes, they are here and alive," we were told.

In the rear corner of the concrete shelter, we found Freily in frightful condition. Her head was half covered by a huge bandage, all bloody and dirty. One of her eyes was rimmed by black and blue circles. Her silk suit was worn and torn, and her grayish hair was matted to her forehead.

"Freily, what happened to you?" I asked.

With tears in her eyes, she told us that just before the last attack of the Russians, she had gone into the antechamber of the shelter to diaper the babies. At that moment, there was a terrible explosion. She remembered instinctively pulling the babies under her body before she fell and lost consciousness.

She later discovered that a hand grenade had been thrown at the iron door of the shelter to blast it open as the Russians stormed in. They found her covered with debris, fallen head-long on the table, with one baby under her body. Her head was bleeding heavily, but the baby was safe. As the troops pulled her out, they were advised by the tenants that there was another baby with her. The Russian, who loved children, ordered the tenants to search through the ruins for the remaining child.

As the tenants were removing a big piece of fallen ceiling, they heard a very faint cry underneath the table. Sure enough, there was the other baby, covered with debris, but alive! He had been pushed under the table by the air pressure, and that's how he was saved. He could barely breathe, since his mouth and nostrils were filled with dust. They cleaned it as much as possible, but he had a terrible panting cough and his crying was like that of an old man. The child needed immedi-ate medical attention, but there was no doctor. Finally, they found a doctor, but he wouldn't come out of the shelter. The patient had to be brought to him.

The Freily had swiftly gathered the child into her arms, enveloping him in his once elegant fur coat, and started to run with him, jumping from doorway to doorway, seeking cover under balconies. The fighter planes were active again as she headed towards the shelter where the doctor was located, but she made it safely there. The doctor diagnosed the baby's condition as severe bronchitis but said the child would recover. He cleaned and drained the child and gave him medication. It was a miracle. Freily hopped back with him from door to door with deep gratitude in her heart. She happily embraced "her" baby, not caring any more about herself. Of course, by this time everyone knew they were Jewish boys, and she didn't have to tremble about that anymore. The devilish house-commander had been arrested by the Russians and presumably executed.

"You are a real hero, Freily," my wife said with a look of admiration. "You risked your own life for these babies."

She passionately embraced the babies.

"Oh, you don't know what they meant to me," she said. "They gave me the courage to fight. They needed me, and therefore, I had to survive. I shall never forget being torn away from my own dear mother, and I was determined not to let these babies suffer the same fate."

She bent her head forward and started to cry. We tried to console her. We told her she would surely be rewarded for everything. Then we asked her to tell us her own story.

"Are you really interested?" she asked, and when we assured her that we were, she continued. "I was a little girl living in a Polish village with my parents, brothers and sisters. One evening, when my dear mother put me to sleep, I noticed that her face was unusually apprehensive. I even asked her, 'Mommy, why do you look so anxious?'

" 'Nothing, my dear,' she replied. 'Just some bad news came about our enemies. They are always ready to hurt a Jew.

But go to sleep now, and let's hope for the best.'

"Later that same night, we woke up to the sounds of screaming, shooting and wild yelling. I remember the horrified faces of my parents as they dressed us in a hurry and told us to run with them out into the dark night. I was trembling and shivering from head to toe as we escaped from our warm little house and ran behind the gardens towards the dark and giant forests. I saw houses aflame like torches, and I heard the horrible sounds of that pogrom as we were pulled by our parents ever further into the woods.

"The old trees of the forest were awesome and frightening. We would never have entered the forest at night if not for this pogrom. We couldn't see as he stumbled through thick roots, stones and branches. At one point, I lost hold of my mother's hand and wanted to run after her. However, my foot became entangled in some creeping root, and I fell full length to the ground. I felt a terrible bang on my head and blacked out. In the pitch dark night, nobody realized this, and they all ran further in blind panic, without noticing that I was missing.

"When I slowly regained consciousness, I cried out for my mother. But only the blowing winds and the night-cries of fearsome animals replied. I realized in total horror that I was alone, left behind! I got hysterical and started to cry and run around, deathly afraid. I fell over and over again and was bleeding all over from the bruises. I didn't care. In my craze, I just cried, yelled and ran with my last reserves of strength until I fell to the ground, unconscious. The sun was high in the skies when I woke up again. The instinct for life drove me further to try and find some help, some human life. I just kept going, sometimes in circles, hungry and in anguish, until I spotted smoke coming from a chimney. Utterly exhausted, I approached the house, crying and yelling, arousing all the dogs to bark, and when I reached the fence, I fell and fainted.

"The Polish peasants immediately realized I was a lost Jewish girl. Somehow, they took pity on me, seeing me as I lay there exhausted and miserable. They took me into the house, revived me and gave me food. At first, I acted wildly, like a captive animal. I remembered that I was not supposed to eat at a *goyishe* house, but soon the hunger and human instinct won over my fear and I started to eat and drink whatever they gave me. There, in that peasant house in the woods, I grew and matured with a broken heart, strongly bearing in mind that I was a Jewish child and that I had lost my parents.

"Later, they had to send me to school. In town, I secretly inquired if there were any Jews, but there were none. My inquiry brought new dangers, because somehow the priest found out I was looking for Jews and started investigating who I was and how I had gotten to those peasants in the woods. The peasants were greatly angered and indignantly rejected the insinuations of the priest, insisting vehemently that I was their niece. The priest was silenced, but nevertheless, the peasants took me out of the school and forbade me to leave the house. I grew up in virtual slavery, secretly crying at night and bemoaning my terrible fate and my fading resistance to this strange life. I suppose they loved me in their own way, and I felt grateful that they had saved my life. I showed them respect and affection and kept my weakening original feelings very deep in my soul.

"They started to trust me and take me visiting, and I made friends in the villages around us. The time came for me to get married, and one gentile boy after another was suggested as a possibility. I saw the inevitable coming, knowing that once I made this step, all my secret hopes of finding my family and my people would be gone forever.

"This gave me the initiative for my strategy. I decided to play along with them up until the last possible minute. After some reasonable selecting and wavering, I selected a prestigious gentile young man from the next town and became engaged. During the preparations for the wedding, I systematically strived to get some money of my own. I saved on every purchase, whenever they would give me money. I even managed to find the key to the cabinet where my dowry was kept and removed small amounts. For my plan, I needed financial independence. Finally, the "big day" came, and I was taken to town by my step-parents for the civil marriage. The judge solemnly gave me my marriage certificate, and when my step-parents wanted to put it away, I told them emotionally that it was my treasure and I wanted to keep it.

"Then they started to cook and prepare for the church wedding. All the relatives began arriving in horse-drawn wagons adorned with flowers. The night before the big occasion, I locked myself in my room and told everyone I was going to bed early. In reality, I put on a dress I had prepared for this purpose and changed my appearance with face lotions and hair dyes. After midnight, a dilapidated wagon pulled by a lanky donkey, stopped at the edge of the forest, and a dark shadow hopped into it, before it continued its voyage on the winding farm roads.

"I was that shadow. The wagon belonged to a gypsy from the nearby hills, my only trusted ally. I'd known this particular gypsy for years, since he came from time to time to fix things in our house. The gypsies were not allowed to live among the population, only in tents on the mountainsides. As a result, they had sympathy for those who were oppressed. By the time the first rays of the sun came up, we entered Krakow, the big city which I had never been allowed to visit. I directed the driver to take me to the Jewish section of the city to the rabbi's house. There I paid him the huge amount of money I had promised him, and he quickly disappeared. It was as much in his interest as in mine that no one should know about this trip.

"On that morning, it was quite difficult to get into the rabbi's house, but my determination was so strong that I was granted an audience after waiting for a while. My story was met with much consternation by the rabbi and his wife. They were shocked and frightened. What would they do with me now? How would they help me and hide me without arousing suspicion and precipitating, Heaven forbid, another pogrom? After all, I had escaped from marrying a gentile, and he would surely search for me far and wide. By that afternoon, it was decided that I couldn't remain anywhere in Poland, for sooner or later the police agents would catch me, and this would place the entire Jewish community in danger.

"Through some special connections, I was sent to Czechoslovakia. I was taken over the border by a peasant who owned land on both sides of the border. From there I was taken to a Jewish community, where I was received with the warmest possible sympathy. They hid me for a while, obtained Slovakian Jewish documents for me and gave me a basic Jewish education. As soon as I was settled a bit, I started working so as not to be a burden to anyone. My Polish identity was hidden, but I still kept my Polish marriage license in a secret place, just in case. It later saved my life.

"In Slovakia, I lived by working to support myself, but in the back of my mind there was the constant feeling of want for having lost my family. I could never outgrow the panic of having been left alone on that awesome night. Being somewhat settled, I made it the purpose of my life to discover my family's fate. I began a systematic search for them. Every penny I earned above bare subsistence was spent on agencies in Poland, Austria, Slovakia and the rest of Eastern Europe. The international Red Cross and the League of Nations in Switzerland were all contacted, but without a trace. The years went by while I frantically searched for my family. I reached the age of an "old maid," but I refused to marry until I found my mother.

"Then the Hitler era came. First the Sudetenland and then Poland collapsed, and I knew that this eliminated the last hope of finding my family alive. Soon, the shadow of anti-Semitic terror engulfed Slovakia, and I watched as the deportations approached my beloved Jewish community. I knew that those deportation trains were heading back to Poland, and the danger for me was worse then it was for them. There I could meet with two deaths, one as a Jew and one as a Christian escapee. I could not risk that. I realized the only escape for me was to resume my Polish-Christian identity.

"Even though the idea of pretending again to be a Christian hurt me, I visited the Polish consulate in Bratislava and applied for a Polish passport as a refugee, using my Polish papers and marriage license as evidence. By that time, no one was officially looking for me in Poland, and I received my Polish passport within a few days. With these identity papers I went to Budapest and took jobs as a nurse for these past two years, until Hitler arrived here. That's how I got connected with your family. They knew I was a Jew, and my perfect Christian identity was security enough for them to entrust their baby boys, camouflaged as girls, with me. They knew they could trust me as long as I lived.

"So that is my story, and that is why I didn't want any harm to befall these innocent little babies."

She bent her blood-covered head over "her" babies, and we felt she would never find that motherly feeling which she'd been searching for since that night in the forest.

How to Survive a Survival

■ ■ ■

Sarah Holczler

IN JANUARY, 1945, AFTER THE RUSSIANS "LIBERATED" BUDAPEST, the city was in shambles. Where stately buildings had once stood, bombed-out shells remained, with jagged solitary walls pointing skeleton fingers to the dark gray sky. The marks of the furious house-to-house battle between the Germans and the Russians were everywhere. The Allied forces, bombing with almost total precision, completed the devastation.

Those of us who survived the unending horrors of the war crouched in cellar shelters as the fierce fighting raged above our heads, staring into each other's faces, trembling and praying. The double dangers of perishing from bombs or from Hungarian Nazis eternally accompanied us. On one occasion, when the shelter walls were swaying from the very closeness of bomb explosions, the head nun ordered everybody to kneel and recite a Catholic prayer.

When we were finally released from our shelter and stepped out to the street, we almost fell over the blackened, dead bodies of Russian and German soldiers and innumerable civilians, men, women and children. The snow on the ground was dark with frozen patches of human blood. The electric wires from poles were down; debris and desolation were everywhere.

Our first thought was to look for our family. But where were they? Had they survived? As we approached the inner city, carefully stepping between human bodies and debris, our bodies, weakened from starvation and constant fear, were hardly able to carry us. From the direction of the ghetto we saw crawling masses of human bodies wriggling on the frozen ground. Blackened skeletons were making a last effort to get out of that hell. We were witnessing the opening of the ghetto. Even among the ruins, this sight was unforgettable. Coming closer we saw naked human bodies stacked in pyres, in endless rows, and living ones were on crutches or crawling.

All our thoughts centered on getting away from the horror and trying to find some human life. We trudged further towards the inner city to the address of my sister. Even if we couldn't find her in her spacious apartment, we were clinging to the hope of obtaining some information about her whereabouts.

Upon arriving at her apartment, we climbed the steps of her unbelievably untouched building with our last effort. We knocked on her door. Our repeated knocking brought out a Hungarian Nazi who, in response to our inquiry, roughly barked that it was his apartment and that he had nothing to do with any previous owner. With that, he slammed the door in our faces.

We were left standing there, longing for a place to settle and rest. We were truly forlorn. Going back to the street, an angel materialized in the form of a Jewish Russian officer. He approached us with a smile, encouraging us by speaking in Yiddish. He asked us what we were doing there and if we were having any sort of problem. We explained our situation, how upon finding my sister's apartment occupied by a gentile, we now had nowhere to go. He told us to follow him. We climbed the stairs again with hopeful expectations. He gave a few rough kicks to the door which promptly opened, showing the gentile face, now fearful. The officer informed him that we were the rightful owners of the apartment and that he had to vacate the premises immediately. He motioned us to sit down while he supervised the evacuation. Within a short time, the man left with his belongings, which we first scrutinized to determine whether he was taking anything belonging to my sister.

To our delight, the furniture and bedding were still intact. When the Jews were herded into ghettos or escaped, which my sister had done, the gentiles took over Jewish property as if it were theirs.

This was our first taste of postwar existence. Our hearts overflowed with gratitude for the Russian *Yiddishe Neshamah* who had come to our aid when we were in such dire need.

At last, we had a place to sleep, but what about food? It was very cold, and the big porcelain fireplace was empty of burning material. My husband went down to the street to look for some wood, and he met many other people doing the same thing. Among the debris, they found broken pieces of wood which he carried upstairs. When the first flames came to life in the fireplace, we almost danced with joy. I wished my sister was with us. What would she say about having us installed in her apartment? Who knew where she was?

The next day dawned upon us. Hunger gnawed at our stomachs. The stores had been bombed out, and no food came into the city from the country. Our meager supply of old, moldy crackers was rapidly disappearing. Water had to be carried from a distant well, and who knew if it was contaminated?

We rearranged the beautiful bedroom set. Moving the

mirrored chest, I suddenly glimpsed a potato sack behind it. My heart stopped from the shock of the discovery. Pulling it out, we saw, to our amazement, a half sack of walnuts. What a wondrous miracle!

After a few days, we couldn't hold ourselves back. We had to find my sister. We met someone who gave us hazy information as to the whereabouts of my sister and other members of the family. They were supposedly hiding over the Danube River on the Island of Csepel. We were warned that it was still dangerous territory with some pockets of sporadic fighting between the Russians and Germans. Nevertheless, we embarked on the trip to locate them.

My husband made a makeshift sled out of wood. This was to be emergency transportation for me, in case I could not walk the whole way because of my advanced state of pregnancy. We were secretly hoping to locate a food supply from the outskirts of the city, since we would be nearer to the countryside.

We must have walked miles in the high snow when we saw a large horse-drawn wagon going in the general direction we were heading. We waved to the driver, who pulled in the horses for a stop. He took us on. By then, our sled which I had used a couple of times, was broken. He gave us a ride for a few kilometers and then put us down.

As we continued, a little refreshed from the ride, we arrived at a large building where trucks were lined up. Too late, we realized we had arrived at a Russian compound. As soon as they noticed us, the leader hailed us, "*Davay! Davay! Ide syuda!* (Come here!)"

They grabbed my husband and led him to the rear of a huge truck. They motioned him to put his shoulder up against a slide attached to it. A heavy sack slid down, cascading onto his shoulder. He was then ordered to carry it to a nearby warehouse.

Seeing my pregnant state, they motioned me to go sit in

the truck's cab. I was comfortable and warm, but my heart went out to my husband, who in his undernourished state was carrying endless sacks, each of which appeared heavier than his own weight. I searched my mind for what to do. After a while, I let out a scream.

"*Moy rebionok! Chlabcy, moy chlabcy!* (I am with child! I am with child!)"

I bent over my stomach, seemingly with pain of my coming delivery. The Russians became panicky. Hastily, they sent my husband to me, even helping put our sled together with a few nails, just to get us away from them. After this experience, we were on the lookout for Russians.

It was night when we finally arrived at the island Albert Falva where my sister was hiding. Our joy knew no bounds to be reunited at last with my only sister and a few family members. We gave them a report on the apartment in the city. My sister could not believe her ears. As we expected, they had some food. After our strenuous trip, we were glad to eat.

We spent a tense night. In the early morning, we all started out towards the city. Our makeshift sled was given over to the children, and we pulled them over the ice and snow. Once, we dropped a sleeping child in the snow and discovered her absence minutes later. We hastened back and found her in the middle of the street, innocently sleeping in the snow.

We arrived at the Danube River which divided the island from Pest. There, a Russian-manned ferry was commuting between the two parts of the capital, Buda and Pest. All the bridges connecting the two parts of the capital had been blown up by the Germans. We begged and pleaded, pointing to our freezing children, until they finally let us onto the ferry. Navigating between ice floes, we finally reached the bank of Pest.

Arriving back in Budapest, we all trooped into my sister's apartment. We were joyous upon accomplishing our goal of bringing my sister home to her rightful residence. As there was no place else for us to go, we all stayed, happy with the cozy knowledge that we were finally united. However, we had no food. Expending mighty efforts, we were able to exchange our meager personal property for bread or any kind of food at the marketplace. It kept us from starvation.

When we found ourselves jealously watching what other members of the family were eating, we knew it was time to get out on our own. No matter how nobly we shared every tiny morsel, we had to consider the little children and their meager rations of life-sustaining food.

My husband and I started out again on the snow-covered streets, taking along three walnuts, which we had discovered in that blessed sack, as our most precious treasures.

I was eight months pregnant.

We headed towards the east, with the ambitious goal of reaching Nagyvarad (Oradea Mare), about four hundred kilometers away. Previously, in the course of serving in the Hungarian work brigade, my husband had escaped from the guards many times and sneaked into the town of Nagyvarad, where he had experienced the hospitality and generosity of their richly laden tables and warm *Yiddishe* atmosphere. Now, my husband wishfully dreamed that this noble, Jewish *kehillah* had escaped harm, since the city was on the border between Hungary and Romania.

So we trudged on. We signalled and pleaded for a hitch on any lorry or truck we saw. I made sure I was highly visible by standing out in front, hoping that my pregnant state would invite sympathy. After several of those hitched rides, we came to small town. I was frozen, numb and painfully starved.

It was dusk. We saw a Russian officer walking on the sidewalk. Recalling the nice experience we had with our Jewish Russian soldier in Budapest, I walked over to him begging, "*Chleb* (bread)."

His stern face broke into a smile, and to my joy, he spoke in Yiddish.

"Listen," he said. "On the next street is our canteen. Go over and ask for bread. I am an officer of the army, but since I am Jewish, I have no power." I felt the bitterness in his tone. "Try it and good luck!"

We took his suggestion, and very soon, I was roughly but kindly handed a good chunk of black bread. It was the best tasting "delicacy" we had eaten in a long time.

When it came time to find quarters for the night, we simply knocked on a door and declared loudly that the Russian officer had sent us to sleep over. The old couple living there grudgingly relinquished primitive day beds. All night, we heard them muttering angrily in the next room. The old man laced each sentence with loud spitting, probably aimed in our general direction.

In the general chaos, people were moving everywhere, hitching onto anything that moved in order to get to some other destination. In that atmosphere, our own movements seemed natural and normal. Not so natural and normal was my pregnant state or our hunger! The gentile population, remaining in their homes, had stocked up on food well before the air raids began. They had never lived like us, like fearful fugitives. When they were closed up in air raid shelters, they fed lavishly on their hoarded goods. They also had no *kashrus* problems.

From time to time, we got bread. In rare cases, we even got a little jam on our bread. We drank hot or cold water and nothing else. So the days passed by.

I became weaker and weaker from constantly walking in freezing weather. Our destination, Nagyvarad, seemed unreachable. What if I were to give birth on the road? It puzzled me that I did not feel any life in me. I doubted that my baby was alive.

Still, while we were hiding and running for our lives in constant, deadly danger, I gave thanks to Hashem that I had the baby in me.

Since I was very thin, the extra weight I carried highlighted my pregnancy. It saved me from being raped. It helped to direct some sympathy towards me. It was a blessing.

At one of the stations, when I couldn't move anymore, I declared "bankruptcy." I just could not continue anymore. My husband was desperate. What would become of us, stranded in a gentile home, where beneath the friendliness we clearly felt their hatred and impatience to get rid of us?!

The next morning, studying a map, we estimated that we were about a hundred kilometers from Nagyvarad, if we would only be able to find a straight line of transportation there. Upon inquiry, my husband found out that a freight train passed through the small town's station. Nobody knew the timetable, as nothing moved on schedule. Since passenger trains were non-existent, we took whatever was moving in the general direction in which way we wanted to go, happy to avoid more trudging in the snow. To our dismay, it was a flatbed freight train, and the climb up was a maneuver almost beyond me.

It was very cold. The destination of the freight train was about forty kilometers from our goal. I remember wearing a pair of men's trousers we had "borrowed" from our last hiding place, also an overcoat, a thin dress and some gloves. We had five Romanian soldiers for company. They could not have cared less about us.

We figured it would be about two or three hours riding time. The fact that the freight train did not have any protective siding made us fearful of falling off when it lurched and changed tracks. Shivering, we huddled in the middle of the train bed. The soldiers, clapping their hands and beating their thighs, suffered the cold with us. One of them tried to ignite a fire in the middle of the platform, but the wind blew it out. It started to get dark and unbearably cold. Our empty stomachs could not produce enough fuel to warm us.

After crawling along very slowly, the train arrived at an elevation which exposed us to cruel, unprotected wind on both sides of the track. I felt numb and very, very sleepy. My husband constantly tried to keep me awake. I knew it was the end. To my horror, I saw the engine of the train become disconnected from the freight cars, leaving us stranded. I watched it become smaller and smaller, a diminishing black drop on the horizon.

I started to cry, but my tears promptly froze. I wanted to sleep forever.

I must have slept. Nothing could keep me awake anymore. Hope was gone. After a long while, I awoke to hear my husband screaming into my ears, "It's coming back! The engine is coming back!"

Somewhere on the edge of consciousness, I felt a stirring. Trying to focus my half-closed eyes, I saw a black spot on the horizon, and it started to grow. The little black speck was growing and growing. Suddenly, my life force returned, and I wanted to pull it faster and faster. The chugging sound became louder, and with this sound, the frozen veins in my body started to flow with hope for life. There was a mighty lurch. We were connected again!

The soldiers hooted with pleasure, clapping and dancing. After a while, we pulled into a small station with illuminated windows and promising warmth.

I had no feeling in my legs when my husband lifted me off the train. As he placed me on my buckling legs, the desire to relieve myself, which hadn't bothered me throughout our long journey, arose suddenly. I stepped away from the train to relieve myself in the dark. Something crunched under me. I had broken through an icy ditch! I fell into it, submerged up to my shoulders. I screamed and screamed until my husband pulled me out and dragged my thoroughly soaked body towards the building.

I only remember a glaringly hot stove, and people jumping from their hard benches to make room for me. I fell onto one of the benches and lost consciousness. Never in my life had I slept so well. In the morning, I awoke bone dry and refreshed on that hard bench. Later, I realized Hashem' wonder. In my frozen state, the icy bath revived me and saved me from frostbite. Still, I did not feel my baby.

The sun was shining brightly when we finally ended our exodus and reached our destination, Nagyvarad. The melting snow became sparkling crystal rivulets flowing alongside the sidewalks. Freshly washed red roofing tile added to the cheerful mood. Beautiful buildings, untouched by the ravages of the war, were a healing sight for our eyes, holding forth a promise of rejuvenation and hope.

However, our eyes were mostly attracted to the food displays in shop windows. We couldn't feast our eyes enough on the wonder of real food, not cardboard. Behind the glass were freshly baked rolls, bread, pretzels and chocolate.

"Where do the Jewish people live?" we asked a passerby.

With a puzzled expression, he directed us to Szacsvay Street. We hastened our step. We found a building with its door wide open. Inside, in the dining room, young men jumped up from a long row of tables to greet us with a warm *"Shalom Aleichem!"* We saw only young men; not a single woman was present. Soon, the steaming meat and potato dishes arrived. I had to fight back my tears of happiness at finally arriving among our own people. We ravished our meals, pausing only to answer to a few questions.

We hadn't filled our stomachs for a whole year and had never seen meat, except for *treif*, which we refused to eat. But that was in the past. At the moment, we were sitting and feasting on platefuls of delicious, steaming kosher food, and we gorged ourselves to the limit.

Our next concern was where to live. One of the leaders of the group, all of whom were returnees from the camps, volunteered to show us around as there were plenty of empty apartments.

Our joyful exhilaration shortly turned into heartbreak. We

were led into fully furnished Jewish homes, rows and rows of them, all empty. Many were lavishly furnished with built-in *sukkos* and *mikvaos*, all standing empty in the ghostly atmosphere. One could almost hear the desperate cries of families, babies, as they were dragged away to be killed.

The Jews of Oradea Mare had suffered the same fate as the others all over Europe. The apartments had been stripped of all personal property. Only furniture remained. And the *mezuzos* on the door frames.

As night approached, we had to choose a place to sleep. Finally, we were persuaded to take one of the rooms. I was sure we would not be able to sleep there, but exhaustion took care of us and we did.

We were the first Jewish couple in Nagyvarad, and we were offered an important job–to be the managers of the Jewish hospital. The job included a one-family house on the hospital grounds for the manager's residence. Very soon, we were established in that house.

The Nazis had stripped the hospital of all furnishings, medical equipment and supplies. It became a shelter with only mattresses, first aid equipment and a few instruments all supplied by the Joint and organized by the young men. I was appointed to receive the returning deportees for disinfection, feeding and generally helping the *Fluchtlings* (refugees) from all Transylvania. A large kitchen was organized. There was one doctor and a handful of orderlies.

In the interim, I gave birth to a healthy baby girl. Hashem's unending *chesed*! She was the first Jewish child born in Nagyvarad after the war.

As time progressed, groups of refugees arrived in unbelievable shape, starved, lice-infested and skeletal. We were notified by the police of each impending group arrival and would wake up early to get ready for them. Our expectations were so high that perhaps we would find someone from our own family in the columns of sickly and tired skeletons.

"But why the police?" I asked. "Are we in a *lager* state?"

I was told that it was because in almost every group, Nazi capos or SS persons were hiding, hoping that by dressing in the *lager* uniform they would escape detection. And indeed, we witnessed arrest after arrest, as the *Fluchtlings*, feeling secure for the first time, pointed out the criminals to the waiting police.

I was assigned the women returnees. We helped them in every way we could. After delousing, they received clean, new outfits, warm food and loving words. To see the first gleam of happiness in their faces as their sores and bruises were cleaned and bandaged was very, very rewarding.

In the next group, to our joy, we found my cousin's twin son, a fourteen-year-old boy whose twin sister was still missing. Of course, he became our boy.

One group arrived towards evening. In it, was a very young girl. The group that had previously arrived was still in the hospital. They lined up, curiously awaiting the newcomers with hopeful expressions. The young girl peered into the awaiting group of *Fluchtlings* and suddenly gave a heart-rending shriek.

"Joszi!" she screamed. "Joszi!"

The young man ran to her and embraced his little sister, cradling her almost lifeless body in his arms. Overwhelmed by emotion, she passed out. We carried her in first, trying to revive her. She was utterly emaciated and without any strength.

"Joszi," she whispered and fainted again.

The doctor couldn't spend too much time with her, as hundreds of others awaited his help. I spent the whole night with her, massaging her heart and forcing little drops of milk into her white lips, trying to keep her alive. The deep, happy emotion had totally strained her weakened heart. When the sun broke through the dark night, she started to breathe a little more regularly, and slowly, she fell into a deep sleep. Another soul was saved.

When my daughter was three months old, a new group arrived from the *lager*. To our amazement, a twelve-year-old girl was carrying in her arms a tiny baby girl of about two or three years old. There had never been any children in the previous groups. I ran to her and took the baby from her sagging arms. As to my question, she answered that she was a twin, and the baby girl was also a twin, but neither of their siblings had survived. They had come from the infamous Mengele's experiment *lager*. She had cared for the little girl like a true sister although they were not related.

The older girl was placed in a shelter, and I took the baby home. The girl was extremely grateful to be relieved of her charge as she was in a very worn out state. The daughter of a *shochet*, she was eager to get away, hoping to find her family and home. We learned the baby's name.

Our lives took another turn. Here was this malnourished little girl, with a big, bloated belly, sores all over her body and skinny legs on which she could not stand. Her beautiful, big sad eyes looked at us, but she never cried!

The twelve-year-old girl who had brought her in was still at the hospital health station where she was slowly recuperating.

"Why doesn't the baby ever cry?" we asked her.

She explained that in Mengele's camp the terrorized children were threatened that anyone who cried would be killed. Even the littlest ones understood the peril of crying. Everyone, even a baby, has the instinct to survive.

I wanted to keep this little girl who showed improvement every day. With careful, slow feedings, her bloated belly went down, and a little more color came into her tiny face, but never a smile or a single tear.

The daily chores were mounting. More and more people came from the *lagers*, two or three groups weekly. We had more accommodations and more medical help, but we lived with much more turmoil and strain.

The story of the little girl staying in our house began to circulate among the new Jewish arrivals in the town. Some of them had been residents of Nagyvarad before escaping.

After the baby was with us for about three months, one member of the Jewish group came to us and inspected her. He inquired whether we had tried to find her parents. How could we? Where were the mothers of little children? The answer was tragically the same all over Europe. They had all been killed, often with their babies.

"Well," he said. "It is still your duty to try and find out for sure whether or not they are alive. It is very noble that you decided to keep the baby, but the parents come first if they are still alive." He then suggested putting an ad in the local newspaper, giving the name of the child and requesting information as the whereabouts of her parents.

We realized that he was right and proceeded to publish our request in a couple of papers. To our utter amazement, after a few tries in various publications, we received a letter from the mother of the child!

Our excitement mounted sky high, but we were afraid to believe this miracle. There were desperate mothers returning from the *lager*, tragic survivors with irreparable broken hearts, emerging from the burning hell where their children had been killed, seeking solace for overwhelming grief. Such a woman would gladly grab any child and hold him close to her heart. We wanted to make sure that the writer of the letter was the child's real mother, so we requested that she provide an accurate and detailed description of her daughter. This she did, and the true identity of the baby was established without any doubt.

Still, we wondered why the mother was not rushing to take her child. Later, we understood that she had lost her husband and all her other children at Auschwitz and was too sick to travel so far. Therefore, we arranged a meeting place at a railroad station closer to her.

While preparing for the trip, my life took another turn. I became ill with milk fever and was unable to travel. My husband took the baby girl and travelled with her to the appointed destination. I was disconsolate, parting with the baby and not being able to meet her mother. Still, we gave thanks to Hashem for giving us the *zchus* to be part of this wondrous miracle.

In the meantime, Nagyvarad became Oradea Mare, officially Romania, and the groups of refugees became more sparse. As the influx tapered off, we made plans to repatriate to Budapest.

The readjustment to life in Budapest, which was still a war-torn city, took all our energy. It was a struggle to make a living, and I was newly pregnant. Later, we emigrated to the United States.

As our children were growing up, I often found myself wondering what had happened to our little "adopted" girl.

Thirty years later, we were residing in a little *Chassidic shtetl*. Every *Shabbos* afternoon, we used to congregate in the living room of a friendly widow. It became a social center for us, which made our hostess very grateful. It eased her loneliness, as she was childless. Many times, she told us how all week she lived for the moment when her room was filled with our company.

On one of these occasions, a lady guest speaker began to speak about a well-known *Chassidic Rebbe* in Brooklyn with a large family who always chose his daughters-in-law for their quality, *midos* and character. But one of them stood out for her beauty of *neshamah* as well as her noble looks. Her *mitzvos* and *maasim tovim* towered over all the women in her circle. She had been miraculously saved from Mengele's infamous twin *lager* for children. A twelve year old girl, the daughter of a *shochet*, who was also a twin, brought her out of the hellhole. Then, she was taken to a Jewish home in Nagyvarad where a family nursed her back to life. In this place, she somehow was found by her mother.

I was on the verge of fainting by the time she finished speaking. I had finally received my long-desired answer about the missing link of our lives. I couldn't hold it back anymore.

"What miraculous *hashgachah* has brought such a beautiful answer to a question deep in my past!" I blurted out with tears in my eyes.

Immediately after *Shabbos*, I prepared to travel to Brooklyn. I had to meet my "adopted" daughter. I had to make sure it was not a dream.

Finally, we came face to face, and I looked into those big, soulful eyes which hadn't changed since childhood. The emotion I felt is indescribable. She was a tall, slim, graceful lady who smiled at me knowingly. She had already heard about me and was planning to meet me. She thanked me with great warmth and gratitude for the care I had given her as a sick child.

But I was grateful, too. My husband and I had truly been blessed. So I gave thanks to Hashem for the *zchus* of choosing us to be instrumental in helping this treasure of a girl become a noble wife and a mother of Jewish children.

A Firebrand Lives

■ ■ ■

Moshe Holczler

IT WAS *EREV ROSH HASHANAH* AGAIN, THIRTY-SIX YEARS LATER, an awesome and serious day, a day of examining one's deeds to find some merit before the Heavenly Court. In general, I felt that, as the generation that survived Auschwitz, we couldn't be judged as any other generation. But still, I searched for something specific, something more outstanding to be presented on the imminent Day of judgement.

I was tense and uneasy because precious hours had passed and still no solution. My son knocked and brought in the mail. Among the letters was a colorful foreign postcard. It had come all the way from Sydney, Australia.

"Look at it!" I exclaimed. "It's Yinghi! Yinghi Braun! We haven't heard from him for so long!"

My son was puzzled, because he never heard of Yinghi Braun.

"He was the first member of our family to return from Auschwitz," I explained. "A young boy who suffered a lot and saw even more. He was the first to tell us what really happened to our parents. Today, he works for El-Al Airlines and is stationed in Australia. What life doesn't produce!"

"With love, Yinghi, Ariela, Ud and Amichai," my son read the signatures out loud. "What funny names these Israelis have."

"Funny? I wouldn't call it that? And if you would know his story, you wouldn't call it that either!"

At that instant, my mind suddenly lit up. This was it! This was the story for *Rosh Hashanah*!

I asked all my children to gather on the porch in the fading rays of the sun, and I told them Yinghi's story.

After the war, a group of refugees arrived at our receiving center in Oradea Mare. The former Jewish Hospital was transformed into a shelter, with the help of the Joint, to receive, disinfect, heal and nourish the starved and exhausted survivors of the German extermination camps. These refugees were swarming home on freight cars and trucks in the weirdest clothing, heading towards the towns that were once their homes in the hope of finding someone alive. They came with hair cut short, with faces gray, with bodies full of lice and bloody scratch-marks, depressed and apathetic.

At that time, I was the manager of a receiving shelter. I had to interview them and help them become fit to continue to their destinations. A day did not pass without someone meeting relatives not thought to be alive. One boy who found his only sister reacted with such a hysterical outbreak that it seemed as if the stone walls were crying. Another time, a middle-aged mother found her daughter in the form of a walking skeleton. We had to be tough to stand it, but it was impossible to be strong enough. My wife would see my red-rimmed eyes day by day and ask me when I would find someone from her family.

Then, on a seemingly quiet afternoon, a thin, surprisingly young boy in a flat cap caught my attention. He was standing alone among a group of new arrivals, sad and soft-spoken. I asked him his name and was surprised to hear the family name of my wife. His hometown was in the vicinity of my wife's town. I proceeded to ask him if he knew her parents. Then I saw for the first time a faint smile on his face.

"That was my uncle," he said.

Hearing this, I ran to my wife to tell her. She could hardly control her excitement, and in seconds she was out there to meet him.

"Yinghi, my dear," she burst out. "Is it really you?"

Her meeting with him was extremely emotional. She just couldn't believe what he had said about Auschwitz. We took him into our home as our own child and nurtured him with our caring love. But it took weeks and weeks until he could bring himself to talk about his experiences.

We learned that Yinghi was alive because he and his twin sister were subjects of the German medical tests in the so-called "twin-lager" established by the infamous Dr. Mengele, the medical "selector" of Auschwitz. Mengele wanted to discover the secret of how and why twins were born so that he could multiply the "superior" German race sooner by making them produce more twins.

Not only were the twins left alive, but being they were so young their mother was also allowed to live. She was sent to a nearby work camp to take care of her twins after work hours.

The special camp for the twins was in the immediate vicinity of the crematorium where, day by day, before their eyes, hundreds of inmates were led to their final destiny. Their brave and devoted mother, widow even before the deportations, fought with her last strength for the survival of her twins. Every day, she would secretly bring them her own food ration to keep up their strength. As a result, her own strength ebbed, and finally, a few days before the liberation, she died of exposure and starvation at the age of thirty-six. She died in the arms of her daughter and was buried at the roadside by the twins, for whom she had given her life. When Yinghi arrived at this point in his narrative, all of us just broke down and couldn't talk for many days and nights.

Weeks passed without Yinghi talking about any of his experiences in the camps or in the twin-lager. Then, on a quiet afternoon in the last week of *Elul* 1945, I had the urge to ask him the big question.

"Tell me, Yinghi," I said. "When you think of everything you went through, what made the biggest impression on you? Something out of the ordinary that you will never forget?"

Apparently, he had been waiting for his question, for he started to answer right away with a low and sad voice.

"The night of *Rosh Hashanah* in Auschwitz," he said. "We kept track of the Jewish calendar, no matter what, and we knew of its coming. Somehow, we had a secret hope that on that day everything will stop, and the Day of Judgment would frighten off our murderers. And behold, on *Erev Rosh Hashanah* it was quiet, surprisingly quiet, around the gas chambers.

"By then, the big transports from Hungary were finished and the only 'business' was the mixed transports of fugitives recaptured from all over the Nazi domain, from the ghetto of Budapest, the forests of Poland and Slovakia, from camps, from bunkers and hideouts. Also, as a regular routine, there was the weekly burning of the living skeletons who were no longer useful in the labor camps. On this *Erev Rosh Hashanah*, however, even this was stopped, and we thought that it might be due to fear of the oncoming day.

"Then, as the night of *Rosh Hashanah* set in, we realized all our hopes were futile. These murderers were the most cynical sadistic beasts of mankind! The other twin inmates called our attention to activity near the ovens. Soon, a detachment of SS men took up positions, and we heard the yelling of the *kapos* as they began unloading a big transport which had just arrived. With horror, we realized that it had been purposely timed just for this night!

"Many men and women and some children started to file out for selection in the night, something almost always done by daylight. In the blinding rays of huge reflectors and among the frightening barking of bloodhounds, they were confronted with Mengele, standing there in his leather boots as if he were the boss over life and death on that *Rosh Hashanah* night. Most were sent to the left with deathly pale faces, because by that time they already knew what it meant. After the selection, the left line was left standing there in the formidable glare of the flaming cremation ovens; we saw their flickering shadows on the ground. One could see on their faces that they knew they would soon be going up in those human-flames.

"We turned away with helpless anguish, when all of a sudden something unusual happened. An elderly man with a beard and a haggard stature broke the silence and raised his hands.

" '*Ledovid mizmor...l'Hashem ha'aretz umlo'ah, tevel veyoshvay bah*,' he exclaimed with a loud, penetrating voice. 'To Hashem belong the earth and its entirety, civilization and its inhabitants.'

"His enthusiastic outcry entered the marrow of our bones, and we saw the whole line of victims shudder at the sound of the holy prayer of *Rosh Hashanah*. With determination and defiance, they joined loudly, word by word, religious and non-religious, old and young, reciting this holy prayer together. Soon it became an open declaration of alarmed souls once more raising their heads and shielding themselves with faith. The SS men were stunned and didn't do anything. Even they understood that this was a last prayer. It became a loud outcry, glorifying the might of G-d in the face of destruction." At this point, Yinghi's entire body was shaking. "I will never forget this, and will make sure my children will not forget it. Perhaps this is I why was left alive."

"What are the names of his children?" my children asked.

"Ud and Amichai," I replied. "Now you realize why these funny names? They are exact reflection of his feelings. He felt himself to be an *ud*, a firebrand saved from the flames, and his only consolation was that *ami chai*, his people were alive!"

On that *Rosh Hashanah*, we presented the message of Yinghi, Ud and Amichai to the Heavenly Court, and we were sure that it would be accepted.

Epilogue: Although Yinghi told us about the *Rosh Hashanah* night, he still refused to talk about Mengele and the twin-lager. For over forty years, he kept his silence. During this time, he moved to Eretz Yisrael, and Yinghi Braun became Kalman Bar-On, a distinguished executive with El Al Airlines.

In 1984, preparations began in Israel for the fortieth anniversary of the liberation of Auschwitz which was to be commemorated the following January. A special committee was set up to organize an international gathering, and at the same time, an all-out drive was made to alarm the world that Dr. Mengele was still at large, unpunished and living off the profits of an international dope ring somewhere in South America. The organization of an all-out manhunt was made the chief aim of the forty-year anniversary. The hitherto limited hunt was now to include the governments of the United States and Germany. The Ad Hoc Committee summoned surviving twins from all over the world to tell the world exact details about the horrors of their suffering.

Yinghi, too, was summoned before this committee. He still couldn't bring himself to the point of talking publicly about the most suppressed torture-memories of his life, but now he had a guilty conscience and felt that he too must help alarm the world to act against that Satan, Mengele.

Finally, when he was approached by the West German weekly *Der Spiegel* and was confronted by their columnist, a *giyores* who converted to the Jewish faith in New Zealand and came to live in Israel, he opened up. Yes! He wanted this German media giant, which reached Germans by the millions, to carry his message about Dr. Mengele to the Germans and awaken such a human furor that even the Germans would hunt their infamous criminal. His interview took hours and hours and he mailed us copies of these. My wife and I both read it and we became sick in the depths of our hearts.

We now understand why Yinghi kept quiet for forty years, what piercing shrieks resounded in his ears the whole time. Every night for long months, he heard the crippled and the sick and the lost babies thrown alive into an open fire, because they couldn't walk by themselves into the gas chambers. He saw Mengele playfully pet a small Czech twin, the favorite of the twin ward, just to cut him to pieces a half hour later to study why a twin is born. He saw how Mengele shoved his lacquered boot into the abdomen of a pregnant woman, for whom he had previously ordered a special milk-portion, and afterwards induced her to have a bloody miscarriage, while he brutally butchered her up with her embryo. He recalled the daily deranged moanings of men whose groins were cut up and their testicles removed without any painkiller or mercy. He saw twins sewn together, their veins connected, wallowing in pain, while he coolly watched their daily progress.

Yinghi finished his letter to us with the following questions: "What would I do if Mengele were finally caught and could face him? Would I cut him to pieces? Would I torture him? No, all that would not be enough!

"Instead, I would confront him with my two sons, Ud and Amichai, and I would yell to him. 'You see, you foolish dirty Satan! You thought you would finish us all and no one would be able to tell the world what you did. But we survived, and this should be your punishment before you are annihilated forever. Ud and Amichai defeated you and your boss, and they are the ones to stay for all time!' "

The White Armband

■ ■ ■

Moshe Holczler, from *Late Encounters*

IT WAS A QUIET SUNDAY AFTERNOON IN APRIL, 1944. WE JEWISH forced laborers were quartered in an abandoned horse stable on the Hungarian plains.

The idea was very firmly entrenched in our minds that we belonged to the royal army of Miklos Horthy, the Regent. There were no more furloughs following the German take-over of Hungary on March 19, 1944. In spite of the disturbing news about the Jewish population of Hungary that found its way to our ears, our minds were clamped into the basic mental attitude that we were no longer individuals but army members and nobody but our commanders had any jurisdiction over us. We didn't fear the Germans, either. We were sure they wouldn't touch us.

Sunday was the only day when we were freed of our jobs filling tank traps and deep trenches which the Yugoslavians had dug against the Hungarian enemy. We wore civilian clothing, with yellow stripes on our left upper arms and army

160

caps on our heads. Our commanders were regular soldiers, and a strict discipline above us made us feel that we were indeed regarded as soldiers. We eagerly awaited these Sundays to rest, clean ourselves, mend torn clothing and do some laundry. We sat on straw sacks laid on the concrete floors and enjoyed a little fresh air mingled with the strong smell of horse manure. Some of us got homesick and wrote postcards to our beloved ones at home.

This was the prevailing mood on that Sunday afternoon as we peacefully mended our clothing while we sang our little songs, isolated from the outside world where civilian Jews in the cities were already branded with yellow stars about their hearts, ghetto walls were erected all over and Jews disappeared from railroad stations, trains and streets, never to be seen again. We just did not realize what was going on.

In the mid-afternoon, an unexpected turn of events disturbed our quiet rest. The word was passed that the doctor of the squadron wished to come in and talk to us. This was very unusual. Although a Jew and a forced laborer like ourselves, Dr. Aurel Stein was generally unpopular, because he was always on the side of the superiors, standing at the side of our officers during command salute in the evenings. He would check us if we didn't feel well, and it was his opinion which determined whether somebody was allowed time off from work. And now, he was going to come in and talk to us on a Sunday, when even our gentile officers didn't dare bother us. What was going on here?

Soon, the door of the stable opened, and Dr. Stein walked in. He wore his usual jacket and army cap, and the Bilgery boots only officers were allowed to wear, which made him even more disliked by us. But the most conspicuous aspect of his appearance was that instead of wearing the usual yellow armband, which until now made him equal with us, he now wore a white armband with a small red cross on it, showing him to be a medical person. We opened our eyes wide with surprise and expectation. What would come out of this?

At his request, some husky boys pulled two heavy stable containers to the front and turned them upside down, making a makeshift stage for him.

He climbed on top and signalled to us to stand up. Very unwillingly we obeyed, because the whole thing irked us and because no official person was at his side. Still, none of us had the courage to challenge him openly.

He was pale and very serious looking as he started to talk in a rather subdued tone.

"Boys, I know it is very unusual that I should talk to you," he began, "but our officers felt that I was the only one who actually comes from your ranks and who could make this talk half official and half not.

"I don't know if you fully realize what's going on with our parents and families all over the land."

At this instant, all of us were electrified. We realized something dramatic was in the works. All eyes focused anxiously on Dr. Stein, now that he had identified himself with us to a certain extent.

"You are kept more or less uninformed here, as this is the proper status for a soldier," he continued. "But now, with the German intervention in our land, you must know what's going on. Our parents and relatives are being concentrated in ghettos, a revival of the ancient hatred against the Jews. There are serious rumors that they will be forcibly removed from Hungary and taken to unknown destinations. What else awaits them there we don't know, but I have to leave it to your imaginations."

At this instant, he stopped and bent his head with a sad look. We stood there fear-stricken and beset with anxiety. Then he raised his head again and continued.

"Boys, we can't do anything about this tragedy. We cannot forget that we are an integral part of our royal army and as far as your own persons go, as long as you are within the army, nobody else has jurisdiction over you. But still, even here in the army, we are already treated differently from regular soldiers. No one knows what additional degradations are waiting for us. Therefore, I have to tell you something now which is very hard for me to say. But still, you have to get this offer, rather, this chance to save at least your own interests."

He stopped for a few minutes, and we looked at each other, bewildered. What does he have in mind?

"His high honor the Prince Primate of Hungary is offering us a helping hand," he continued with grave significance. "The protection umbrella of Christianity."

He had to stop for a few minutes, because the open consternation was reflected in our eyes and many of the boys broke out in a half audible hiss.

"Boys, be patient," he continued in a voice of soft persuasion. "I know how you feel, but you have to be very somber in this situation. The holy Church guarantees safety from any further deportation procedures to anyone willing to enter its ranks and be baptized. Those who accept the loving hand of the Church, which is really a very generous gesture, will receive a white armband and will be transferred to an entirely different squadron, together with me. Now, boys, whoever is interested has to contact me in the days to come, and I am authorized to arrange your conversion. I know that such a decision cannot be made at once, but please think it over and don't be hasty in your decision. I don't think you will have another such offer. Now, does anybody have any questions in this respect?"

He looked around, but all of us were standing there with our eyes fixed on the floor and a general murmur of indignation filled the stable. Still, after a few minutes, one of the huskiest boys, the leader of our work unit, raised his hand and asked in a subdued and trembling voice.

"Do you think that by doing that there is a chance to save our parents and families?" You could hear in his voice that he had to overcome a deep resistance to ask the question, just for the sake of our families.

The answer came in a drawling voice from the doctor.

"No, I don't think so," he replied. "But at least we could save ourselves."

And thus, he stepped down from the makeshift stage and left the premises with hasty steps, before any trouble would break out in his presence. After he left, a frozen silence filled the stable. Everybody was stunned and confused. After a while, the expected storm broke out.

One of the most outspoken boys, an absolutely modern and rude country boy, was the first to respond.

"A rat!" he spit out. "And a disgusting one!"

"I always hated him," another one retorted. "I saw that he was no good. Such impudence, to dare to induce us to leave our religion, just to get some advantage from it! He changes his faith like his clothing."

The air was filled with similar remarks of indignation and exasperation. They turned their anger on the unit leader who had asked the sole question.

"How did you even dare to ask him such a question?" he was asked. "That he should think for a minute we would cooperate?"

He was pale and worn as he answered.

"You know I would never do it for myself, no matter that I am not religious at all," he defended himself. "But I figured that maybe for the life of our families we would have to sacrifice."

"Our parents would never want this from us," another yelled loudly. "This would be treason, spinelessness, and a dirty mess."

The entire quarters was brewing with excited emotions as the eight of us, the "kosher group," stood in a corner and watched with enthusiasm the behavior of our non-religious comrades.

Rudy, our leader, couldn't keep from exclaiming, *"Mi ke'amcha Yisrael?* Who on earth is such a people as Your people Israel? You see, none of them is ready to jump ship, none of them is willing to leave the path of his forefathers, even for his own safety!"

No matter that they eat non-kosher, no matter that they hardly keep anything, they still refused to deny their origin even in this hour of danger.

Sure enough, as the days passed, nobody but nobody accepted the "helping and loving hand" of the Church and nobody became "white armband exempted."

Dr. Aurel Stein disappeared from there for good, probably fearing he would be beaten up by us. He left behind a deep-seated loathing and disgust, and our squadron continued its fateful path with even more resoluteness and pride. The kosher group didn't fail to praise them and to tell them that they reached the highest level of sanctification by their firm rejection. Dr. Stein was not seen again for a long, long time to come.

Times became more dramatic every week. Nobody cared anymore about saving a Jew. At the peak of the deportations in June, our company was alerted and taken to the Ukrainian front. Two weeks later, they were caught in a cross-fire between Russians and Germans on top of a hill and out of two hundred, eight survived.

The "white armband exempted" detachments were moved to an unknown location, and we didn't hear about them again.

After the final storm of the war and the liberation by the Russians, those with the slightest life instinct managed to leave the country. An emigration followed to all possible parts of the world, and some of us arrived in America and began new lives. New struggles and new worries occupied us in the new world, and we almost completely forgot our forced labor experiences.

It happened thirty five years later...I was returning from a visit in Flatbush, Brooklyn, a very exclusive section of quiet streets, elegant mansions and lavish lawns. On one of the corners there was a prestigious public building of yellow-faced bricks and a *magen david* on its upper edge. It was a branch of the Young Israel. As I passed by, my eyes involuntarily ran over the framed blackboard standing on two galvanized posts. It gave the timetable of the daily and *Shabbos* services, and underneath, the following text was written out in plastic lettering: "Attention. This coming Thursday night our guest speaker will be Dr. Aurel Stein, the prominent humanitarian physician. His topic: Judaism Superior. Don't miss it!"

I came to a sudden stop, because some bad feeling took hold of me. What a familiar name. Where had I heard it before? But why did I have such a bad feeling about this name?

As I was wondering and searching in my memories, suddenly that red-head with the Hungarian army cap and that left arm with the white stripe stuck in my mind. Yes, he was Dr. Aurel Stein, the rat and the traitor who offered us Christianity to save our lives. But what a coincidence that this should occur to me in Flatbush at the announcement of a program about the superiority of Judaism!

I continued my walk engulfed in my unpleasant memories and was already half a block away when somehow I felt an urge to turn around. Motivated by curiosity and an irresistible urge, I discovered that my legs were carrying me up the front stairs of the Young Israel building, and soon I was knocking on the office door. I received a friendly "Come in!" and there I was at the information desk.

"Well, I saw your sign outside about your program on Thursday night," I said. "Somehow, this name is very familiar to me, and I don't know where to place it. Could you please tell me who this Dr. Stein is and where he lives."

The receptionist directed me to a secretary who was a little puzzled by my inquiry, but then readily told me that this man was a very respectable doctor. He was very active in their ranks and did a lot of good for members of the Young Israel.

"Many times he cures them free of charge," she said, "And he takes part in every worthy drive for the promotion of Jewish culture and interests."

My surprise became stronger with every word, and finally, I came to the point. "And may I ask you where he is from? Is he an American?"

"No, by no means," was the reply. "He came from the old country about thirty years ago, and if I am not mistaken, he must be a Hungarian. He still has a strong accent, and I heard he comes from Budapest."

I could no longer contain myself. I became red from inner excitement and increased heartbeat.

"I am almost sure this is my man," I said. "Could you give me his address and telephone number?"

The secretary became a little irked.

"Sorry, sir," she answered. "I would have to ask my superiors for permission. And may I have your name and address before I do that?"

For a few moments, I hesitated. If he was really the same person, and if he found out I was looking for him, he would surely hide from me. So what would I accomplish? Wouldn't it be better if I appeared on Thursday night and identified him for myself beyond any doubt? This was the right path to follow.

I didn't give her my name, which fact she acknowledged with a sarcastic smile, and soon I was on the street again.

On that Thursday night, I appeared in the auditorium of the Young Israel to wait for Dr. Aurel Stein. Then, exactly on time, the side door opened and in walked an elderly man clad in a dark blue suit. As he took his place at the lectern, a few people who knew him stood out of reverence, but the audience was mostly seated. I was the only one who jumped up, with a tremor. I tried to hide, and gazed with eyes popping out at the lecturer. I almost couldn't suppress an excited yell: Yes, this was he! After thirty-five years, the same Dr. Stein, but in a much older form, with white hair and eyebrows, with a rather stocky posture and this time with a *yarmulke* on his head instead of the army cap and the white armband. The discovery was astonishing. I had to marshal all my self-restraint to control myself. I wanted to hear what he would say before I made any conspicuous or offensive move.

The man started to talk, and I fell from one surprise into the other. Before my ears and eyes, a very talented and self-assured, highly educated Jewish lecturer unveiled himself, full of genuine Jewish enthusiasm and sincere thoughts of the highest caliber.

I was so fascinated and mixed up, that I was just sitting there incapacitated and bewitched. I waited until the end, and I was still sitting as the people, after a warm ovation and repeated congratulations, started to file out of the room. I let them clear out, and finally, it became obvious that I purposely stayed behind. At that instant, the secretary, who was surrounding the doctor with a group of Young Israel leaders discovered me, and I saw her whisper something to one of the executives. Eyes started to scrutinize me, and somehow the lecturer's attention was directed also towards me. This was already very unpleasant, and I had to get up and approach the group in the front. I started to smile to hide my embarrassment and turned with explanation to one of the managers.

"I am sorry to disturb you," I said, "but I think I discovered in the doctor somebody from the old country?"

This moved him to smile cordially, and he turned around to Dr. Stein to tell him that some gentleman from the audience seemed to know him personally. I saw the puzzled smile, mixed with a little hidden fright, in the eyes of the lecturer, as he reached his hand towards me.

"To whom do I have the honor?" he asked in a strained voice.

I decided that by no means would I shame him. Who knows what changes had happened in his life since?

"I think I know you, doctor, from Hungary yet," I said to him in a friendly voice.

He wrinkled his eyebrows, as one searching in his old memories. "Really, and where from?"

"At this moment, I don't know exactly," I replied. "But it would be so nice if you would give me a chance to see you personally in your office, if you would give me an appointment."

He was surely relieved as he caressed his forehead with a little tremor in his hand.

"Oh, surely, why not?" he said. "Here is my card. Call me at your convenience for an appointment." Then he raised his voice. "It will be so nice to bring back old memories." Then he turned to his company. "Gentlemen, it's kind of late, and I am a bit tired. Maybe we should part now for a friendly meeting again."

It took a few days until I decided to call him for a personal appointment. His voice was a bit irritated again, as he asked me on the telephone.

"But who are you?" he wanted to know. "And where did you see me?"

I told him frankly and sincerely where I knew him from, and I perceived the very unpleasant surprise in his voice. I assured him I was not here to hurt him and that I was very deeply interested to know what happened since I had last seen him.

At this point, his behavior changed.

"Not only will I let you see me, but I definitely want you to see me," he retorted. "Let's choose a leisure time when I could talk to you and tell you a lot of things."

Finally, the appointed day for that private interview arrived. It was a quiet afternoon in late summer when I faced Dr. Stein in his study at his mahogany desk, surrounded by deep leather sofas and numerous shelves on the walls, filled with books of medicine and science. By contrast, above his head was a separate shelf for Hebrew books, sets of *Mishnah, Gemara, Shulchan Aruch* and the works of the Rambam. It all gave the impression of an established religious Jewish doctor.

"Please tell me now how you remember me from Hungary," was his cautious initial proposal. "Then ask your questions."

"Look, Dr. Stein, I have to tell you honestly that the contrast is quite great," I started with a nervous inflection in my voice. "The last time I saw you was in a forced labor camp when you appeared with a white stripe on your arm instead of our yellow one and offered us the "helping hand" of the Catholic Church, openly calling upon us to convert in order to safeguard our future. And I also must tell you openly that you were the object of universal hatred by all of us, even by the non-religious boys of our squadron. And now, after thirty-five years, by sheer coincidence, I encounter you as a lecturer on the superiority of Judaism. It's obvious I had to put all my self-control in gear not to exclaim and unveil your past before I asked for an explanation for this turnaround."

"I really appreciate that," answered the doctor. "And I hope you will believe that my present activities can only stem from thorough conviction. Nobody in this world would expect it from me or force me in such a direction."

Then he began his story in a soft, explanatory manner, many times, however, barely suppressing his deep human feelings wishing to erupt from behind the barrier of self-control.

"When I left your squadron and was transferred to a white armband exempt squadron of fellow-converters, stationed near Esztergom, the seat of the Prince-Primate of Hungary, I was quite mixed up in my feelings," he began. "I was disappointed in my Jewish upbringing, seeing the fiasco of it and witnessing the collapse of all Jewish institutions in Hungary.

Was this the answer to all our struggles for the Hungarian homeland? Was that the fate of my diligent studies to become a doctor? Where was the heavenly protection for us, the so-called Chosen People, which I heard repeated by religious leaders again and again? I had to see how our parents and families were herded together like cattle and forcibly thrown out of Hungary to be killed.

"Then, a few months later, I was informed that your squadron was taken to the Ukrainian front and perished in a crossfire between the Germans and the Russians, despite the fact that you refused to save yourselves by converting. So what should I have felt? Out of total disappointment and desperation, I went to the other extreme. Maybe they were right, I thought. Maybe we are an inferior people who only suffer persecution and murder throughout human history.

"I had had my fill of being the oppressed Jew and decided to approach my new milieu, not so much out of conviction but rather gratitude for saving me and out of common sense, to get out of this mess alive. My family, who would have reproached me, was dead anyhow, and after the liberation, I appeared in Budapest as a gentile physician, making a nice living from private patients who came to me after my hours at the people'sclinic. I diligently observed the ways of thinking of gentiles and wanted to assimilate myself to the best possible extent.

"But my interest did not let me stop halfway. I wanted to see and understand everything in Christianity. That's when I decided, a few years later, to make a trip to Italy, to see Rome and to visit the Vatican, which remained the center of my new gentile world, even after the Communist expansions.

"On a hot summer day, I arrived in Rome at the entrance to St. Peter's Basilica in the Vatican. I was kind of proud of that magnificent building, surrounded by elaborate arcades on both sides of its plaza. What a difference! The Jews are always crying about their two-thousand year old ruins, while we have a beautiful central palace of Christianity which was never attacked and was earning the reverence of the entire world!

"Then I entered the cool chambers of the Church, full of historical and artistic masterpieces. I have to admit, though, that it was kind of strange and uninviting, as I read the names of the Popes buried in the walls of the Cathedral. What an idea, to put graves into the walls of the house of prayer! The aggressive smell of incense was also unpleasant, but I attributed it to my own immaturity on my road to Christianity. Everybody had to file into a long line as our guided tour led to the raised statue of the apostle Peter sitting on a bench covered by his long robes with his right foot sticking out of the gown. It was of bronze and was supposed to be very holy. Everybody filing by had to kiss the end of the toe, which just reached the height of our mouths. It was shiny from the constant kisses, in contrast to the other parts of the statue which were tarnished into a dark bronze.

"As I approached I felt a kind of disgust to kiss it, because as a doctor I couldn't imagine licking the saliva of hundreds of people. I felt everything but holiness. So when my turn came, I nicely imitated a kiss and humbly proceeded further.

"Soon we arrived into the innermost chamber of the Basilica. The steady boom of an organ was heard, and the scent of incense was chokingly mixed with the smoke of hundreds of long, giant candles that were lit around an oval opening in the floor. People were kneeling all around it and engaged in deep prayers. We were told that over there was the holy grave of St. Peter himself. Nuns were endlessly turning their long prayer chains as they recited their lamenting songs.

"Then we arrived at the Papal Throne, made out of pure gold. It was empty now because the Pope was at Castel Gandolfo for his summer vacation. But as we turned to our left, our attention was called to a gigantic statue, which practically filled the elevated dome of the chief section of the Basilica. It was a standing angel with spread out marble wings from its back, from one end of the circular dome to the other.

"Our guide was telling us that this marble angel was the foremost artistic work of Michelangelo, the great sculptor of the Renaissance, and it was unrivalled in splendor. Really, I had never seen such a giant artistic statue in my life. As I inspected it for myself more carefully, I discovered that it held something in its marble hands, stretched out and pointing towards the raised Papal Throne. I realized that it was a big, flat marble tablet, and something was written on it in shining gold letters. Their forms were strange, and I couldn't make out what was on them. Seeing my strained glimpses, a Dutch tourist offered me his big binoculars. I gratefully accepted and focused on the marble plate.

"I was taken aback. I was startled to discover Hebrew letters on it and instinctively shuddered, wondering if anybody else had seen it. Then I started to read it slowly, using my long-forgotten Hebrew knowledge. '*Onochi Hashem Eloke-cha*. I am G-d, your Lord.' The first of the Ten Commandments! And this was facing the Papal Throne forever, held by the giant angel. I got such a stinging sensation in my heart that the Dutch tourist was startled by my paleness. Without a word, I gave him back the binoculars, and while he started to look at the object of my consternation, I quietly and rapidly sneaked away and made a frantic effort to get out of there as unnoticed and as quickly as possible.

"On the hot Basilica plaza, I stopped in the shadow of the arcades and ran my hand over my forehead in anxiety. So this is all their knowledge? To base their entire religion on the Jewish revelation of Divinity? And they have to put this in their holiest place? Why then should they be considered superior to Jews? And why should they hate the Jews if they cannot deny them, even in front of the Papal Throne?

"My entire frame of mind was shaken. I was confused and upset, and my mind started turning the clock back in my soul at a stormy pace.

"A few days later, I arranged for a visit to the Jewish Chief Rabbi of Rome and asked him for some information about the history of Rome's past. To my utter surprise, he informed me that I could see some utensils of the destroyed Holy Temple in the Vatican Museum. I wasn't lazy and easily gained entry into the museum with my gentile passport. There I discovered some utensils of the ancient altar, the golden angels of the holiest of the holy places and when I saw the golden forehead-plate of the *kohain gadol* engraved with the words *Kodesh Lashem* (holy for the sake of G-d), somehow my heart constricted. I had to discover for myself that I was still a Jew in my heart, no matter what happened and what I did. Upon my inquiry, the superintendent priest of the Vatican Museum informed me that still more could be seen in the British Museum of London, where many items seized and looted by Titus were kept.

"The next year, my trip to London followed, and my irresistible reversion back to Judaism increased. I was longing to know everything of the Jewish past, but still I didn't come to the decisive point of returning officially to the Jewish faith. Then, a year later, a trip to Israel followed.

"My feelings as I approached the pastel outlines of the shores of the Holy Land were a sensation unto themselves. I was puzzled at how I was overcome by sentiments to the utmost. Then, two days later, I arrived at the mystical Jerusalem and wanted to visit the remnants of the Holy Wall of the *Bais Hamikdash*. There, something happened to me that I cannot understand until this very day.

"As I approached the Wall, my throat constricted, and my eyes fogged. I don't even know how I got into such a state. I only know that I threw myself onto the stones and clutched my ten fingers on the crevices of the age-old rocks. Then a hysterical weeping gushed out of me and rocked my entire body. I never imagined I could cry and shake so vehemently and so loudly. I didn't know what was going on inside me. I just felt that my soul was being born anew. When I finally managed to utter some words, I asked forgiveness for what I had done and promised everything I could if I would be accepted back again.

"On the same day, I approached the Chief Rabbi of Jerusalem with my problem, and I returned to Judaism, never to part again."

When he came to the end of his story, his eyes were full of tears, and so were mine. I had no more doubt as to how he came to the point of sermonizing about the superiority of Judaism. That marble angel had shown him the way!

Those Little Shoes

■ ■ ■

Moshe Holczler, from *Late Reactions*

ON A SLUSHY BROOKLYN WINTER MORNING, I WAS ON MY WAY home from *shul* when I happened to stop at the block where my daughter lived. It was the typical Boro Park morning rush that stopped me; many big yellow school buses filled with eager children of different *yeshivos* wildly proceeding to their destination.

I had a sudden urge to stop off at my daughter's home. I turned onto the street and rang the doorbell and was met by the surprised countenance of my daughter. What brought me here so unexpectedly on such a foggy, unfriendly morning? I quickly assured her that nothing was wrong. I simply wanted to say hello and see how she felt.

After offering me a seat, my daughter sighed with visible exhaustion.

"You will have to excuse my appearance and the disorder of my house," she said, "but at least now you see how I start my day, after these little kids leave. Just look! Like a leftover battlefield! No one puts anything away, no one has time. And who is the maid of the house? Mother, of course, who has to rush to prepare breakfast and send along a recess snack and lunch. It's too much! The mess, the disorder, the clothing in the most absurd places. And look at those shoes thrown around! Not one with its pair, some under the bed, some in the corner. It's very annoying."

Looking for sympathy, she glanced at me, only to notice that as I spotted the shoes, I suddenly became sad.

I put my head down and couldn't talk for a few minutes.

"What's wrong?" she asked, bewildered. "Why did you become so sad?"

"Now I understand why I felt such a sudden impulse to visit you this morning," I said in a tender voice. "What you just said about these shoes, brought back a very painful memory.

"It was in late February of 1945 when your mother and I decided to leave Budapest, which had been freed by the Russians in January from the German troops. There was misery and hunger in the war-torn capital of Hungary, because the Russians robbed the city of all its reserves. Women had to barter their wedding rings for a pound of flour, and each surviving member of our family received one piece of bean for the *Shabbos* meal. We couldn't risk such starvation, because your mother was expecting you and had a very strong desire for food. We started out on a snowy morning like today, in our only clothing, walking north on the Vaci Ut. After being picked up by a Russian truck, we began our risky journey towards the inlands, through which the war had passed a half year earlier. One late night, after two weeks of adventures and ordeals, we arrived at our destination, Nagyvarad, a city on the Romanian border, in an open railroad car among many refugees.

"I knew this lovely city from the time of my forced labor under the Nazis. In my memory it was a colorful, pleasant place, where many thousands of warm-hearted religious Jews lived. They were extremely good, neat and intelligent. It was a city of abundance, joy and brotherly love. My heart pulled me to return here, although I knew that the dear faces would not be there anymore. Still, I hoped to find some of them and some traces of the plentitude which had existed there before.

"We waited and slept on the benches until the morning and then set out to see the city. We stopped at the first grocery store. Your mother didn't want to believe that the food displayed in the show-window was real. When we hesitantly inquired inside, an indignant laughter was the answer. We quickly bought fresh rolls, butter, cheese and milk and then left the premises like thieves, checking into the next hotel in haste. We locked the door from inside and plugged the key hole with paper. And then we started to eat! Hot tears flowed down the face of your mother as she ate the first roll with butter. She was trembling with excitement.

"After nothing was left, we set out towards the former Jewish sector to find any returned Jews. To our surprise we found a small group in one of the rooms of the old congregational building. There was a free kitchen set up by the American Joint, where steaming soup and cooking meat welcomed us. The returned refugees surrounded us with such enthusiasm that we knew we had arrived in the right place. Soon some old friends discovered me. They were officials of the old congregation. Hearing that we intended to stay, they embraced us with the greatest of warmth. We were the first Jewish couple to come. And, what more, with a baby on the way! We were served a kingly midday dinner, and our only remaining desire was to settle down. They took us to the nearby Szacsvay Street, in the heart of the former Jewish centrum which I knew so well, to offer a home to us.

"This was our most dramatic encounter with the tragedy that had befallen our people with the deportations. A long street stretched before us with boarded-up entrances, without inhabitants, abandoned for over a year. In the place where hundreds of happy, Jewish children had once run and played, high grass, cats and mice roamed instead.

"After a deep sigh, the former secretary motioned to us. 'Any of these houses can be yours,' he said. 'Whatever furniture you like you can take, anything is yours. Just stay with us.'

"He turned around and left us to make our choice. Our deep desire to find a home was now mixed with sadness and horror. Your mother looked at me with a desperate gaze. 'How can we start a new life on such a ghost street?' she asked.

"The sun began to set, and we needed a shelter. We opened home after home with a crowbar. From the first house we turned away immediately, because children's toys lay scattered on the floor; from the second, because pictures of the family with their eight children were on the walls. By this time your mother's eyes were filled with tears. The third house was plain unfriendly.

"The fourth was more to her liking. It was very neat and orderly, with no sentimental traces. We started to inspect it to make plans. By chance, I pulled away a curtain hanging over a doorway. On a dresser near the window were three pairs of children's shoes–a little pair, the next a bit bigger and the third still bigger. They were nicely polished but now covered by a film of dust, probably prepared for the next *Shabbos* a year before. The shoelaces were neatly made into bows.

"A stabbing pain pierced my heart and tears rushed to my eyes. Who knows where the little feet fitting these neat shoes were? I pulled back the curtain fast, just in time to prevent your mother from looking.

"She saw tears in my eyes and asked, 'What happened?'

"I flatly declared, 'I don't want to stay here or, for that matter, in any of these houses!'

"She saw in me that I couldn't explain why, and I knew that it would be bad for her health and that of her future child. So we returned to the hotel and gave up our homemaking dreams for the time being. During the night, we alternately cried under our bedcovers."

Then I turned to my daughter. "Until this very day, your mother doesn't know what was behind that curtain."

As I finished my story, my daughter quietly started to pick up the shoes from the floor, without a word.

A *Minchah* in the Air

■ ■ ■

Moshe Holczler, from *Late Encounters*

IT HAPPENED ON THE SECOND LEG OF MY FIRST TRIP IN AN airplane. Although many times in the past I have vowed never to allow myself to be carried away by one of these steel birds, I now found that if I kept the corner of my eye glancing frequently out of my round window, I could somehow find security in the silver wings upon which I was actually traveling. I knew it was an illusion, because we were 36,000 feet above the ocean, thousands of miles away from the next shores. Still, the sight of the metallic hardness made me forget the immense void around us. I think it is the same with our religion, which helps us in its well-defined boundaries to grasp the endless greatness of G-d.

The pilot announced that shortly we would reach St. Jones Island, which I knew to be in Northeastern Canada, but so far only the sun seared in through the window on my right, while little fleece clouds appeared beneath us. I was on my way home from Europe via Brussels.

There was not much to note at the airport in Brussels, but just before take-off something happened, which delayed the departure of our plane by a good twenty minutes. Over the loudspeaker came the following message: "Attention Stewardess Suzanne and Steward Peter! Please proceed to the rear and unlatch the emergency door. Let the ramp down via code sixty and stand by the left. Further instructions will follow. Captain Francois speaking." Of course, all eyes turned to the rear as far as it was possible, being that we were already strapped to our seats in preparation for take-off.

In a matter of a few minutes, the door was opened and the ramp lowered. All I was able to discern was that a blonde woman, somewhere in her fifties, was being lifted in on a wheelchair, with an attentive husband hovering over her. The stewardesses seemed to have a problem deciding where to station her, as the aisles were too narrow for the wheelchair. Finally, they hit on a perfect solution and placed her in the only wide space available in the square corridor between the rear emergency exit and the kitchenette. There they somehow secured her and helped her husband tuck a heavy wool blanket around her legs. There were some more instructions from Captain Francois, and the plane was once more shut. Minutes later, we took off.

I shut my eyes trying to get some rest. I must have been very tired, because I instantly fell deeply asleep. The clicking of the loudspeaker woke me. "Ladies and Gentleman! We are now well over land and are beginning to come down the East Coast, on time as planned. However, I have just been notified by Kennedy Airport that the air routes into and out of the airport are unusually heavy and, due to bad visibility, we are asked to circle new York for about an hour. There is no need for concern, since we have ample fuel and even a snack coming up. So try to relax please. Thank you!"

We would have extra time in the air; this was not a very comforting feeling in my heart. Uneasy feelings began to build up in me. To take my mind off my problems, I glanced around at my fellow passengers. Right across the aisle from me sat the man whose wife was in all likelihood that crippled lady in the wheelchair. Our glances met, and before I knew it, we had struck up a conversation. He told me he was coming over to the United States on a medical trip. I did not want to pry, so I kept silent without asking details. I did not have long to wait. Seeing my Orthodox Jewish appearance, he observed me for a while in silence and then decided to talk.

"Take a look at my poor wife back there," he said. "She is the reason for my trip today. We have tried in all of Britain as well as Belgium to find a cure for her legs, but it was all in vain!" He sighed deeply. "When we married, shortly after the horrors of the Holocaust, she was a delicate beautiful girl, with a frail body and weak legs. You see, my wife was dragged as a youngster through several concentration camps and several deep winters. She was torn away from her family who were all killed, and she was left to flounder with the other inmates in the cold in threadbare clothing. The Nazis wanted to experiment to see how long human endurance can stretch. Her torment was worst on her poor feet, because they were forced to work in deep snow and ice with only rags on their feet. Whoever collapsed was shot. So she suffered one frostbite after the other and contracted a severe rheumatism in her young frail bones.

"I married her despite it all, even though I knew she was not very strong. Her tragic beautiful eyes haunted me. They had so much pain and depth! When I married her, she was able to walk, but it got progressively worse. After the birth of our son, her legs went altogether. Now, maybe in the United States, there is a glimmer of hope at one of your great university hospitals." Here he stopped abruptly. "Well, I quite unburdened our life to you, but as a religious man, I figured you would understand."

I tried in whatever way I could to assure him of my deep

sympathy. To everything he nodded silently, but when I mentioned that G-d would hopefully heal, he spoke out again.

"You see, if you bring this up, I have to tell you something more," he said. "I was from a modern background and my wife's parents were Orthodox. But this didn't deter us. After the camps, such barriers fell down. We didn't care and we married. But later, to my great shock, I found out that she was less religious than me! In fact, she had forsaken all religious feelings and turned her back on them. I didn't blame her one bit. In fact, I admire that she has been able to remain so human, so fine in heart, after so much suffering."

Here he stopped and, visibly tired, lit a cigarette. I would gladly have continued talking with him, but he seemed to have withdrawn into his shell.

I left him alone and leaned back to rest and think over the story I had just heard. Suddenly, I glanced at my watch and realized with quite a start that it was *Minchah* time. With the extra delay, it surely would be pitch dark by the time we landed. Even now, when we still had bright sunshine up there, those must have been the latest minutes for *Minchah* down in New York. There was no alternative but to *daven* on the plane. Soon, I realized that a number of other persons had the same thought and were nervously anxious to use the opportunity while the sun was up. As soon as they saw me going around, they rose from their seats one after the other, waiting for further directions.

I didn't want to do anything without official permission. To our luck, near the front of the plane I encountered a man of rank. I asked him if there would be any objection to us getting together into a prayer group for our afternoon services. First, he looked at me with surprise, but something in the earnestness in my voice or eyes must have carried through. He asked me to wait a moment and disappeared into the cockpit. While waiting, I looked back into the cabin.

"Sir!" a voice shortly called. I turned to find the same

official behind me. He paused for a moment, and then in a surprisingly respectful manner, he said, "The Captain says you may pray with your friends in the rear of the plane, so long as is doesn't take long, and it is done in an orderly and quiet fashion. And also," here he paused as if embarrassed, "Captain Francois sends his compliments and asks you to remember him in your prayers." With this he turned and left.

I remained rooted to the spot for a moment. Soon the loudspeaker clicked and a polite announcement was heard: "Some gentlemen asked permission to conduct afternoon services. Whoever wishes to join please proceed to the rear of the plane. We are asking our passengers in the rear seats to move forward temporarily. We thank you for your understanding."

G-d's wonders never cease, I felt. This was already more than I expected. I felt a bit obligated for such an honor.

In a relatively short time, more than a *minyan* gathered. It was as if an electric current had switched a solemn mood into our hearts. We made our way cautiously to the back of the plane, while some passengers, a little reluctantly, moved forward to make place for us. Not all of us were religious, but the drama of the moment was strong. There we were in the air, rushing towards an evening sky, gathering for a public prayer that even those who had not *davened* for years joined us now.

The only place available for undisturbed prayer was the square area designated for us, where the woman in the wheelchair sat. We noticed her bewilderment as we approached, so we explained to her husband that we would try not to disturb her and that the whole thing would take about ten minutes. He reluctantly got her consent. We tried to stand in a group on one side to her left. Of course, we had to turn the other way, corresponding to religious law, but even so, she was very close to us, sitting there practically pinned to her wheelchair. It was a very bizarre situation.

We began the familiar *Minchah* prayer, humming the age-old chant as quietly as possible. Soon, it melted into a mellow tone. Then came *Shemoneh Esrei*, the quiet central prayer.

It was totally silent now, and the swaying movements of the worshippers had a special quality, the quality of a rare moment. All of us felt it. Outside, the sun was setting quickly, sending forth its last glorious colors of mauve and gold. We felt suspended between heaven and earth. We realized that above a certain height the sun is always shining. Regardless of how dark and cloudy it may be on earth below, up above there is a steady calm in the undisturbed world of G-d.

And then a comparison flashed through my mind. The same must be true with our souls as well. If we rise above our worries and desperations, we should be able to find the inner sunshine of our soul, the eternal sublimity of our *Neshamah*.

With this thought, I happened to be the first to take the three steps back out of the prayers. As I stepped back and virtually out of this miniature synagogue, I turned, and my glance unintentionally fell on the woman in the wheelchair who was forced to witness our prayers so closely. What I saw was a drama itself.

Her face was as pale as gossamer, and her eyes were huge with tears unshed. Our eyes met for a minute, and she realized that I had discerned her inner feelings. She closed her eyes, and the tears began to flow uncontrollably. She uttered no sound. She had no need to, because I understood. Her soul had been awakened.

My praying partners were quite disturbed when her husband rushed to her and pushed them aside. They hastily finished the rest of the prayers and returned to their seats. The situation was further misunderstood. Two stewardesses approached with a kind of indignation at the disturbance. But very quickly they were turned back by the couple who declared that everything was all right. The woman asked her husband to calm everyone down and to assure them that nothing wrong was done to her.

I myself was anxiously sitting in my seat, wondering what would come out of this sudden outburst. I didn't have to wait too much longer. Shortly, the husband appeared and politely asked if I wouldn't mind coming over and listening to what his wife would like to tell. Of course, I readily agreed.

She sat with the tears wiped off, but with red cheeks still quite evident and slightly trembling hands.

"Thank you, sir," she said. "Thank you so much. Please, I hope you don't mind, but you surely understand what happened to me. I cannot tell you what a deep memory was revived in me with your prayers. Something from long, long ago, from my early childhood, when I was but nine years old.

"I had become dangerously ill with scarlet fever. My parents saw that nothing was helping and that the doctors were unable to cure it. As a last resort, my father, who was a deeply religious man, was advised that he should change my Jewish name and thus perhaps my fate. I will never forget the sight of the group of Jewish men entering my room and forming a *minyan* at the side of my feverish sickbed. As they said the prayers, the humming of their words resounded in my blood-pulsating ears like a relieving ozone. And with every word they said, I felt I was getting better. An endless gratitude filled my heart, and I felt that my father brought these men to save my life. The next day, I was out of danger, and the doctor said that a miracle had happened. Then, yet a child, I made up my mind that I would never forget G-d who had this power of miracles."

At this instant she bent her head down and began to weep again.

"But I have forgotten G-d," she sobbed. "Perhaps I had reasons to. Look at my misery. I thought He had forgotten me, so I had the right to forget Him, but deep in my soul I knew I was not right. I defied Him, but I knew I was accomplishing nothing by this. But now, when you all gathered around me and hummed the ancient prayers, suddenly a little door sprang open in my soul, a door to that old feeling as I lay feverishly in my bed and the humming sound brought me back from the border of death."

At this moment, she lifted her eyes in which I noticed a detached distant look, despite her outward enthusiasms.

"Your prayers now have brought me back to my faith," she said. "It is good to believe again the way I did in my youth. Maybe there is still hope for me."

She paused for a few minutes and then turned to me.

"Please tell your friends that they should not feel bad for even one minute," she said. "They did me the greatest favor."

I wanted to answer something, when suddenly the flashing seat belt signs appeared, and the captain's voice came over the public address system: "Everybody, please be seated! We are approaching our landing."

Finally! The plane began its descent, and soon we were engulfed in thick billowing clouds. The beautiful sunshine gave way to a peach green, soupy mass. It became completely dark, and soon a misty rain splashed the body of our trembling thunderbird. Surely, we were in New York.

The touchdown was a bit shaky but safe. The usual music began as we were taxiing towards the arrival building. Everyone was relieved that the prolonged landing was ended.

Taking my hand luggage, I turned to say good-bye to the couple, but they didn't let me off the hook so easily.

"Please for one more minute!" said her husband. "My wife wants to ask you something."

"Why do you think this whole thing happened to me now?" she wanted to know.

It was a tough question, and I felt that my answer held the key to her future beliefs. I felt I had to point to the very root as I felt it.

"Because G-d loves you," I said, "and wanted to grant you the opportunity to get back to the mood of the old feeling, which guided you to Him the first time."

The reaction was exactly as I expected. I had hit to the point. She became red again and grabbed her husband with both hands.

"Did you hear?" she cried. "G-d loves me. Did you hear?" And the tears of happiness started to flow again.

The doors of the plane opened, and we started to file out. People were pushing and rushing because of the lost time. But for a few of us this prolonged landing was worth everything in the world. It had produced a "real" touchdown, landing not on the pitch-dark, wet concrete, but rather Up There, where the sun always shines and an eternal beauty reigns.

THE
HOLOCAUST
DIARIES

כָּל זֹאת בָּאַתְנוּ וְלֹא שְׁכַחֲנוּךְ
(תהלים מד:יח)

All this has befallen us
yet we have not forgotten You
(*Tehillim* 54:18)

The Holocaust Diaries is a collection of distinguished memoirs of survivors whose rocklike faith was tested in the fiercest crucible in history, true heroes who emerged stronger than before and rebuilt a new Jewish world on the ashes of the old. (For a more detailed description of the objectives of *The Holocaust Diaries* collection, see Publisher's Note.)

C.I.S. Publishers invites holocaust survivors with similar autobiographical manuscripts to submit them for editorial evaluation. The primary concern is content, not style; our editors are prepared to assist such authors in the process of preparation for publication.